Welsh

Medicine

by David Hoffmann

ABERCASTLE PUBLICATIONS

Contents

First Impression 1978
Second Impression 1979
Third Impression 1983
Fourth Impression 1987
Fifth Impression 1988
Sixth Impression 1992
Seventh Impression 1996
Eigth Impression 2000

Published by
Abercastle Publications
Blaenrhos, Lady Road, Blaenporth
Aberteifi/Cardigan, Ceredigion SA43 2BG
Tel: 01239 811267

Printed by Dinefwr Press, Llandybïe, Carmarthenshire.

The Herbal

Introduction

"... and the fruit thereof shall be for meat,
and the leaf thereof for medicine."

Ezekiel 47; 12

"He causeth the grass to grow for the cattle
and herbs for the service of man."

Psalm 104; 12

This small book is a brief look at the wisdom and practices of the old physicians of Wales. It has not been written with the intention of providing a herbal handbook for modern usage, but to provide some background and insight into the lives of the ordinary Welshmen of the middle ages. On delving into the book you will find that, at least in the area of health, Welsh culture at that time was far in advance of England and Europe. A high degree of care, concern and understanding was shown to the patient, coupled with deep understanding of disease and the plants used to treat it.

The book starts with a look at the history of Welsh medicine from the Druids to the Physicians of Myddfai. The legendary origins of the Physicians, the story of the Lady of the Lake, is followed by a review of modern herbalism, its philosophy and practice. The bulk of the book is taken up by the herbal, a look at the most commonly used plants of Wales, a description of the plant, its modern medical uses, followed by the use the Physicians made of it, and finally any folk lore relating to it.

Ancient
Welsh Medicine

Medicine, 'meddyginiaeth', is said to have been included among 'the nine rural arts known and practised by the ancient Cymry (Welsh), before they became possessed of cities and a sovereignty', that is, before the time of Prydain ab Aedd Mawr, about 1,000 B.C. In that early period, the priests and teachers were the 'Gwyddoniaid', or men of knowledge, who were looked upon as the chief sources of wisdom in the land. As among other early peoples, the priests of the 'Gwyddoniaid' combined the office of healers of the body with that of teachers of the religion.

It is to these men that the inception of the ancient art of healing in Wales is attributed. The three sciences which they chiefly studied were astronomy, theology, and medical botany. The remedies they used were mainly confined to herbs.

During the reign of Prydain, the 'Gwyddoniaid' became divided into three orders, which consisted of the Druids, the Bards, and the Ovates, each of which had its peculiar specific duties as well as privileges. The Druids were responsible for the mystic and religious rites, the Bards for oratory, poetry and music whilst the Ovates for the natural sciences and medicine.

As early as 430 B.C. (before the time of Hippocrates), there is evidence from the laws of Dynwal Moelmud, that the art of medicine was protected and encouraged by the state. In these laws medicine, commerce and navigation are called the three civil arts, each with its own set of privileges. This privilege is stated to have been 'by grant and creation of the judicature, and distinct from the general privileges of a country and kindred'.

It is probable that the Druids and Ovates became acquainted with Greek medicine through the Phoenicians, who traded with Britain, because in later times the name of Hippocrates (the so-called Father of Medicine) is mentioned, and his works were much esteemed by the Physicians of Myddfai.

Druidic medical therapeutics is an interesting combination of mystical and herbally rational techniques. For internal and lingering complaints they mainly used the cold bath, exercise and change of place, with the administration of herbs. Great use was made of water from certain wells, due to their specific mineral and spiritual properties. They devised general prescriptions for the preservation of health in the form of short maxims, commending cheerfulness, temperance, exercise and early rising. The Druids devoted considerable effort to study the medicinal properties of plants, believing some herbs to be endowed with magical virtues. Prominent amongst these was Vervain, used to anoint people to prevent fevers, to procure friendship and to obtain all that the heart desires.

Laws of Howel Dda

Whilst mention is made of medical matters in the work of Taliesin, the 'Chief of Bards', in the 6th century, we must look to the time of Howel Dda to follow the developments of Welsh medicine. Howel Dda, named Howel the Good, was the King of Dyfed about 930 A.D. He laid down a code of laws which was used by the Welsh until the time of Edward the First. One of the laws dealt with the office and privileges of a physician to the Royal Court, with an account of his duties and fees:

(1) The twelfth is the mediciner of the household.
(2) He is to have his land free; his horse in attendance; and his linen clothing from the Queen, and his woollen clothing from the King.
(3) His seat in the hall within the palace is at the base of the pillar to which the screen is attached, near which the King sits.
(4) His lodging is with the chief of the household.
(5) His protection is, from the time the King shall command him to visit a wounded or sick person, whether the person be in the palace or out of it, until he quit him.
(6) He is to administer medicine gratuitously to all within the palace, and to the chief of the household; and he is to have nothing from them but their bloody clothes, unless it is for one of the three dangerous wounds as mentioned before; these are a stroke on the head unto the brain; a stroke on the body unto the bowels; and the breaking of one of the four limbs; for every one of these three dangerous wounds the mediciner is to have nine score pence and his food, or one pound without food, and also the bloody clothes.
(7) The mediciner is to have, when he applies a tent, twenty-four pence.
(8) For an application of red ointment, twelve pence.
(9) For an application of herbs to a swelling, four legal pence.
(10) For letting blood, four pence.
(11) His daily food is worth one penny half-penny.
(12) His light every night is worth one legal penny.
(13) The worth of a medical pan is one penny.
(14) The mediciner is to take an indemnification from the kindred of the wounded person, in case he dies from the remedy he may use, and if he not let him answer for the deed.
(15) He is to accompany the armies.
(16) He is never to leave the palace, but with the King's permission.
(17) His worth is six score and six kine, to be augmented.

If the mediciner was insulted while inebriated, he was not entitled to compensation as 'he knew not what time the King might want his assistance'. He was free to travel the road, and out on the road 'along with the messenger of the sick'. It is also stated that anyone might take another's horse to procure a medical man for a person in danger without having to make amends.

The Physicians of Myddfai

The next authentic account of Welsh medicine dates from the early part of the 13th century, during the time of Rhys Gryg (Rhys the Hoarse), a son of Rhys ab Gruffydd, a great prince of South Wales. He was a fine soldier and took a prominent part in the feuds of the time. Following ancient custom he had his domestic physician, named Rhiwallon, who was assisted by three sons, Cadwgan, Gruffydd and Einion. The family lived in the village of Myddfai in Carmarthenshire.

Under the patronage of Rhys, the physicians made a collection of medical recipes applicable to various diseases of the body 'as a record of their skill lest no one should be found with the skill they were'. Many of the prescriptions can be traced back to the time of Howel Dda, if not sooner. It was the Physicians of Myddfai, however, who collected them and put them in writing for the first time, and thus the valuable record of the medical knowledge of this early period has been handed down to us.

A body of legends built up around the Physicians of Myddfai relating to the magical origins of their skill and knowledge. This is the legend of the Lady of the Lake. Folklorists can trace the pattern of this legend back to ancient times, with the scenario occurring in different cultures and contexts. Let us look at the legend of the origin of the 'Meddygon o Myddfai', the Physicians of Myddfai.

This account comes from the early 19th century rendering, which accounts for the hyperbole in the language.

The Legend of the Lady of Llyn-y-Fan Fach

Near the end of the twelfth century, there lived at Blaensawdde, near Llanddeusant, Carmarthenshire, a widow whose husband had died in the struggles of the princes of South Wales to preserve their independence from the English. The widow had an only son to bring up, and providence smiled upon her so that her livestock increased such that they needed to be grazed on the close-by Black Mountains Their favourite place was near the small lake called Llyn-y-Fan Fach, on the N.W. side of the Carmarthenshire Vans.

As the son grew he was usually sent by his mother to tend the cattle on the mountain. One day whilst walking along the margin of the lake, to his astonishment he saw, sitting on the unruffled surface of the water, a Lady. She was one of the most beautiful creatures that mortal eye had ever seen. The young man just stood still with his eyes riveted on the woman and unconsciously offered her the barley bread and cheese which he had with him.

Bewildered by a feeling of love for the Lady, he continued to hold his hand out to her. She glided near to him but gently refused the offer of the food. He tried to touch her, but she eluded him saying:

"Cras dy fara!
   Nid hawdd fy nala"
	"Hard baked is thy bread!
	   'Tis not easy to catch me"

and immediately dived under the water. The love-stricken youth returned home, desolate that he had lost one, in comparison with whom all the fair maidens of Myddfai were as nothing.

When he had told his mother what had happened, she advised him to take some unbaked dough or 'toes' the next time, as there must be some kind of spell connected with hard-baked bread, 'bara cras', which prevented him catching the Lady.

Next morning, before the sun had gilded with its rays the peaks of the Vans, the young man was at the lake, not to look after his cattle, but seeking the same enchanting vision he had seen the day before. But he waited in vain, the surface of the lake being only graced by the ripples caused by a stiff breeze, and a cloud hung heavily on the summit of the Van, adding gloom to his already distracted mind.

Hours passed and the day became warm and sunny, when suddenly he noticed his cattle on the precipitous slope on the opposite side of the lake. As he rushed over to them, to his inexpressible delight, the Lady appeared once more, more beautiful than ever.

He held his hand out to her, full of unbaked bread, which he offered from his heart with vows of eternal attachment. All of which were refused by her, saying:

"Llaith dy fara!
   Ti ni fynna."
	"Unbaked is thy bread!
	   I will not have thee."

But the smile that played on her face as the Lady vanished beneath the waters raised a hope in the man which stopped him despairing at her refusal. When he returned home, his mother suggested that next time his bread should be slightly baked, as this would probably please the mysterious being with whom he had fallen in love.

Impelled by an irresistible feeling, the youth left the house early the next morning and ran until he came to the margin of the lake where he waited with a feverish anxiety for the reappearance of his Lady. Many hours the youth waited, his flocks of sheep and cows wandering hither and thither, but all his thoughts and attention were directed at the lake for the reappearance of the Lady.

Day was fast turning into night and all hope of seeing the beautiful Lady was gone. The young man cast one last look over the waters when to his astonishment he saw seven cows walking on the water. They were followed by the maiden, who seemed even lovelier than ever. She approached the land and he rushed to meet her. A smile encouraged him to hold her hand and on his offering the bread, she accepted. After some persuasion she consented to become his bride, on condition that they should live together only until she received from him three blows without cause:

"Tri ergyd diachos."   "Three causeless blows."

Should he ever strike three such blows she would leave him forever. But he gladly agreed.

Thus the Lady of the Lake agreed to become the young man's wife, but then immediately darted back into the lake. The youth was desolate, deciding on the spot to end his life by casting himself into the deepest water of the lake that contained his loved one. As he was about to do that, there emerged out of the lake two most beautiful ladies accompanied by a hoary man of noble visage and extraordinary stature but having all the force and strength of youth. Addressing the youth he said that he consented to the marriage provided the youth could distinguish between his two daughters, correctly choosing his loved one.

This was no easy task as they were perfect counterparts of each other. As the young man perplexedly looked at the two sisters, unable to see any difference between them, one put forward her foot and he noticed a difference in the way she tied her two sandals. This he recognised from the Lady he had fallen in love with, and boldly took her hand. As he had chosen the right sister, her father gladly consented to the marriage giving a dowry of as many sheep, cattle, goats, and horses that his daughter could count without heaving or drawing in her breath. He added, however, that should the youth prove unkind to her, and strike her three times without cause, she should return to him and bring back all the livestock.

And so the marriage took place. When the time came for the Lady to count the animals, she counted by fives, as many times as possible in rapid succession till her breath was exhausted. After counting the sheep, cattle, goats and horses, the full number came out of the lake when called upon by the father.

They went to live at a farm called Esgair Llaethdy, about a mile from Myddfai, where they lived in prosperity and happiness for several years, bearing three beautiful sons.

One day they were to go to a christening in the neighbourhood, but the wife was reluctant to go saying the distance was too far to walk. Her husband told her to fetch a horse from the field which she said she would do if he got her gloves from the house. When he returned from the house with the gloves he found that she had not moved. Jokingly he slapped her shoulder with the gloves saying, "Go, go." Thus he had struck her the first time without cause.

On another occasion at a wedding, in the midst of mirth and merriment, she burst into tears and her husband touched her on the shoulder and asked what was wrong. "Now people are entering into trouble," she said, "and your troubles are likely to start as you have struck me a second time."

Years passed and their sons grew to become clever young men. The husband was ever watchful lest he should, in some trivial incident, strike his beloved wife again. She told him, as her love was as strong as ever, to take care for the final blow would, by an unalterable destiny over which she had no power, separate them forever.

It happened that one day they were at a funeral, where, in the middle of great mourning and grief, the Lady was happy and laughing. This so shocked her husband that he touched her saying, "Hush! hush! Don't laugh." She said that she laughed because people, when they died, go out of trouble. She then went out of the house saying, "The last blow has been struck, our marriage contract is broken and at an end! Farewell!"

She went back to Esgair Llaethdy and began to call the sheep, cattle, goats and horses that she had brought with her as a dowry. They all obeyed her call, even a little black calf that had been killed came alive and joined the others. The four great oxen ploughing in the field left their work when they heard their mistress call:

"Pedwar eidion glas	"The four grey oxen
Sydd ar y maes	That are in the field
Deuwch chwithau	Come you also
Yn iach adre!"	Quite well home!"

Away they all went across the mountains towards the lake from which they had come. On reaching the lake they disappeared beneath the water

15

without leaving a trace except the furrow made by the plough drawn by the oxen.

What became of the ploughman when the oxen set off, or what happened to the disconsolate and ruined husband, is not handed down in legend. But of the sons it is said that they often wandered by the lake in the hope of seeing their mother. It happened that during one of these walks near Dol Howel, at the Mountain Gate, still called 'Llidiad y Meddygon', the Physicians' gate, the mother appeared to the eldest son, Rhiwallon. She told him that his mission on earth was to be a benefactor of mankind by relieving them of pain and misery through the healing of all disease.

To this end she supplied him with a bag full of prescriptions and instructions for the preservation of health. She prophesied that if he and his family followed those instructions clearly they would become the most skilful physicians in the country for many generations.

She appeared on several occasions to her sons and once accompanied them as far as 'Pant-y-Meddygon', the Dingle of the Physicians, where she pointed out to them the various plants which grew there and revealed their medical properties and virtues. The knowledge she gave to her sons, together with their unrivalled skill, soon gained for them such celebrity that none ever possessed before them. And to ensure that that knowledge should not be lost, they wrote it down, for the benefit of mankind throughout the ages.

Rhiwallon and his sons first became physicians to Rhys Gryg who gave them rank, lands and privileges at Myddfai. Their fame soon spread and their services were in demand throughout the country. The descendants of this ancient family continued to practice medicine in Wales without a break until the middle of the eighteenth century, when the last lineal descendant died in 1743. The late Rice Williams, M.D., of Aberystwyth, who died in 1842, appears to have been the last of the Physicians descended from the mysterious Lady of Llyn-y-Fan Fach.

Sources

It is thought that the original manuscript of the Physicians of Myddfai is the one now to be found at the British Museum. A number of copies are known to exist, the most important of which makes up part of the Red Book, at Jesus College Oxford. The manuscript consists of 188 paragraphs, including work on anatomy, physiology, medicine, surgery, pathology, materia medica and therapeutics.

The materia medica mentioned in the manuscript comprises about 175 plants, flowers, roots, etc., the list including foxglove, poppy, valerian, peppermint, broom, etc. The preparations of these were generally in the form of infusions, decoctions, pills or ointments.

Another source of information is a manuscript said to have been compiled by Howel the Physician, who was a son of Rhys, who was a son of Llewellyn, who was a son of Phillip the Physician, who was a lineal descendant of Einion. The exact date of this work is not known but it is probably late 15th century. It consists of 815 paragraphs ranging over many topics.

A translation of both these manuscripts was published in 1861 by the Welsh Manuscript Society. The original Welsh and an English version by John Pughe appear. Extracts that appear in this booklet are taken from Pughe's translation.

The Medicine of the Physicians

A careful study of the writings of the Physicians of Myddfai show that the art of medicine practised in Wales in the 15th century was farther advanced, and was freer from the influence of superstition, than in most European countries at that period. Medicines were prepared with care and attention, their properties tested; and attempts were made to analyse the symptoms of disease before treatment was started.

An analysis of the maladies prescribed for gives us an interesting insight into the conditions of the time. The two largest groups of prescriptions are for the treatment of the eye and the skin. This is closely followed by broken bone and wound remedies, then chest and throat cures. Treatments for intestinal worms are numerous, as are remedies for kidney stones. There are few prescriptions for heart illness, for the arthritic/rheumatic diseases so common today. There are, within the works, prescriptions for most things ranging from fevers and painful periods to sleepwalking and insanity! Before discarding such remedies as superstition we should remember that one of the most used drugs in mental illness today, Reserprine, is an extract from the ancient Indian herb Snake root, *Rauwolfia*.

If we assume that the numbers of remedies relate to the medical concerns of the day, a number of interesting conclusions can be drawn. It would seem that illness mainly stemmed from external environmental factors, e.g. smoky houses affecting eyes, worms affecting the stomach, damp unhygienic conditions contributing to lung disease, etc. In addition to wounds inflicted by their fellow men, we cover the bulk of the remedies in this way. Today, it would be fair to say that much disease is due to the internal environment, from synthetic diets, ingestion of very strange artificial food additives and pollutants, etc. The rheumatic diseases, the high incidence of heart disease, all point to something deeply wrong in our personal and social lifestyle. It must also be remembered that much illness today is the result of previous medical treatment; it even has a name: Iatrogenic disease, the diseases of medical progress.

Medical Practice

There is found in the writings of the Physicians a list of the 'Essentials of a Physician'. Included in that list is some excellent advice for the young doctor. He is exhorted to be a kind man, gentle, mild, meek, intelligent, wise and gentlemanly in act and deed, in word and conduct, being careful not to shame those whom he has to examine. The complete list includes much of relevance to the overworked medical man of today!

In addition to the prescriptions direct to the practitioner, some had assumed a wide circulation among the Welsh as medical maxims. These show sound common sense and an appreciation of the importance of good diet and hygiene. These maxims are included in the following pages. The advice and axioms laid down for the guidance of the practitioner prove that the ideal of the early Welsh fathers of medicine were lofty, and their knowledge in advance of the times in which they lived.

The Essentials of a Physician

(13) He should be a kind man, gentle, meek, intelligent, wise and gentlemanly in act and deed, in word and conduct, being careful not to shame those whom he has to examine, particularly when he has to examine women.

(14) He should be skilled in all professional acquirements, and should know the complexion and sign of every feminine disease. He should be able to examine the sick, whether man, woman, boy or girl, in regard to age, constitution, sex and that in a mild, gentlemanly way, both as to address and voice.

(15) He should carefully keep all professional secrets, nor should he divulge them on any account, to any man, nor on any consideration.

He should most carefully avoid intoxication, tippling, or incontinence in any shape, as there can be no trust or dependance upon those Physicians who are addicted to such evil deeds, nor can that respect, which learning and professional intelligence are entitled to, be accorded them. He should be a faithful subject, lest he should practice treachery or treason in the exercise of his profession, on native or foreigner, friend or foe; for the office of a Physician is not to slay, but to preserve with God and His peace, and not with the rage and enmity of man to his fellow man. He should have also his warranted Books of Art authorised by a master, so that he may be cunning in the judgement and science of the wise and skilful Physicians who have preceded him, and who have written with authority in Cymraeg, Latin and Arabic.

A lancet to bleed or open an abscess, also a knife somewhat larger.

A steel or silver spatula to spread plaster. His plasters, his ointments, his pills, his powders, his potions, carefully preserved to meet any demand and occasion.

A garden of trees and herbs, where such herbs, shrubs and trees, as do not everywhere grow naturally, may be kept cultivated, and were foreign trees and plants, which require shelter and culture before they thrive in Wales, may be grown. He should also have his dried herbs, roots, seeds and barks kept at hand so that they may be had in winter, and other times when they are not to be obtained growing, or above ground.

He should also have at hand his honey, wax, pitch, rosen, gums, oil, tallow, grease, lard, marble slab, ale, wine, mead, distillations and other articles as may be required.

Medical Maxims

(from the Book of Iago ap Dewi)

He who goes to sleep supperless will have no need of Rhiwallon of Myddfai.

A supper of apples – breakfast of nuts.

A cold mouth and warm feet will live long.

To the fish market in the morning, to the butcher's shop in the afternoon.

Cold water and warm bread will make an unhealthy stomach.

The qualities of water: it will produce no sickness, no debt, and no widowhood.

It is no insult to deprive an old man of his supper.

An eel in a pie, lampreys in salt.

An ague or fever at the fall of the leaf is always of long continuance, or else fatal.

A kid a month old – a lamb three months.

Supper will kill more than were ever cured by the Physicians of Myddfai.

A light dinner, a less supper, sound sleep, long life.

Do not wish for milk after fish.

To sleep much is the health of youth, the sickness of old age.

It is more wholesome to smell warm bread than to eat it.

A short sickness for the body, and short frost for the earth, will heal; either of them long will destroy.

Whilst the urine is clear, let the physician beg.

Better is appetite than gluttony.

The bread of yesterday, the meat of today, and the wine of last year will produce health.

Three men that are long lived, the ploughman on dry land, a mountain dairyman and a fisherman of the sea.

The three feasts of health: milk, bread and salt.

The three medicines of the Physicians of Myddfai: water, honey and labour.

Moderate exercise is health.

Three moderations will produce long life, in food, labour and meditation.

Who so breaks not his fast in May, let him consider himself with the dead.

He who sees fennel and gathers it not, is not a man but a devil.

If thou desirest to die, eat cabbage in August.

Whatever quantity thou eatest, drink thrice.

God will send food to washed hands.

Drink water like an ox, wine like a king.

One egg is economy, two is gentility, three is greediness and the fourth is wastefulness.

If persons knew how good a hen is in January, none would be left on the roost.

The cheese of sheep, the milk of goats and the butter of cows are the best.

The three victuals of health: honey, butter and milk.

The three victuals of sickness: flesh meat, ale and vinegar.

Take not thy coat off before Ascension Day.

If thou wilt become unwell, wash thy head and go to sleep.

In pottage without herbs there is neither goodness, nor nourishment.

If thou wilt die, eat roast mutton and sleep soon after it.

He who cleans his teeth with the point of his knife, may soon clean them with the haft.

A dry cough is the trumpet of death.

What are Herbs?

What is a herb? To a botanist it is a plant that has no woody tissue and therefore no persistent aerial parts. To a herbalist, however, a herb is any plant material that is of medical value. So we find the roots of burdock being used, the bulb of garlic, the bark of cramp bark, the flowers of elder and the seeds of fennel and so on. A vast store of knowledge of the nature and usage of herbs is available to us. Each culture in every part of the world developed its characteristic herbal pharmacopaeia from Amazonian tribesmen to the advanced medical systems of China.

Historically, the use of herbs can be traced back almost as far as traces of Man. The library of the Assyrian King Assurbanipal contained a clay tablet, dated about 2,500 B.C., enumerating 250 vegetable drugs, many of which are used today. Of the Egyptian Papyri, the Papyrus Ebers is the largest and most relevant. Dated 1,550 B.C., it draws on much older information and contains a materia medica of many plants including wormwood, elder, aloes, styrax and cannabis. The history of herbs in the west can be followed through the development of Greek culture with men such as Hippocrates, Theophrastus and Dioscorides. The writings of these men and Galen, the Roman, are respectfully acknowledged by the Physicians of Myddfai.

During the Middle Ages the countries of Islam were the scene of much activity in the field of medicine. The philosopher and physician Avicena wrote the book 'Canon Medicinae' in 837 A.D. The beginnings of the divergence of what has become orthodox medicine from herbalism was started by the increased usage of minerals such as mercury and antimony by Paracelsus in the 14th century.

It is only in very recent years that western medicine has stopped using a wide range of herbs. In China and India, herbal treatments are part of the total medical approach, being used side by side with the techno-medicine of the west. The World Health Organisation has been asked by the nations of Asia for help in the development of their native medical systems, having now recognised that our exported medicine is not the panacea it was held out to be.

That herbs should have any medicinal value, comes as a great surprise to technological man. We are products of a culture deeply entrenched in a narrow scientific materlialism. The pharmacologists will extract the 'active' ingredients of the herb and then proceed to synthesise it, but any suggestion that the plant itself is of any value is ridiculed.

An Evolutionary View of the Relevance of Herbs

All life on our planet functions as an integrated whole. Through the ecological interactions of all things with each other and their physical environment, life as a whole is maintained on our world. The parallel between planetary ecology and body physiology is evident. This vastly complex mosaic of mutually supportive interactions has evolved over geological time. This process is well summed up in the title of a book by G. E. Hutchinson, 'The Ecological Theatre and the Evolutionary Play'.

The further our science investigates life, the subtler become the strands of interactions we are aware of. The evolutionary appearance of the flowering plants has been a vexing question for many years. In the Cretaceous period (about 100 million years ago), early forms appeared which were members of the Magnolia family. Very quickly they diversified to give the vast range of flowering plants we know today.

From detailed ecological work, it is now evident that the evolution of these plants, the bulk of medicinal herbs, occurred in harmony with the animals feeding on them. Thus, when a new plant evolved the insects would soon adapt to feeding on it, thereby generating a new species of insect. This would produce an evolutionary pressure on the plant species to diversify further, producing adaptations which the insect could not feed on. The insect would then in time adapt and so on. The result is a partial explanation of the driving force behind the evolution of our great diversity of life.

Some of these plant adaptations have been physical, such as the growth of thorns and hairs. However, some plants responded chemically with the production of alkaloid, quinones, essential oils, glycosides, etc. These chemicals have no known physiological function to the plant, and were thought to be merely waste products. With the evolutionary view we can see that they are an essential part of the plant's integration to the environment.

It is these very chemicals that are of such value as medical tools. Many of them are now being used by our pharmacologists. We must remember, however, that Man is a product of evolution, and as such, is it not logical to assume that our bodies are well adapted to the natural environment. Can we not conclude that the needs of our bodies are supplied by Nature, for if not our species would have died out by now? We must remember that the view of nature as 'red in tooth and claw', is far from the truth. Of perhaps greater importance than competition is mutual aid, at all levels, i.e. species supporting species for mutual benefit. From this perspective we can look at the vast flora we share our planet with in a new way, as brothers – co-evolutionary partners, not surprised at their properties but thankful. All our bodily needs are provided for by Nature, food and medicine.

Pharmacology of Herbs

Let us briefly look at the important contribution herbs have made to orthodox medicine. Whilst plants are used as sources of pharmaceuticals, the plant itself or an extract is rarely used today. Alkaloids are plant chemicals found in a large range of plants. Perhaps the most famous is Nicotine, found in tobacco. These chemicals fulfil a number of functions, ranging from morphine and codeine found in the opium poppy, to atropine and scopalamine found in the thorn apple and henbane.

Many of these drug-producing plants have been used for generations as herbal remedies successfully treating the disease that the drug is not intended for. The alkaloid ephedrine, which has led to the development of the amphetamine drugs, is now used in the treatment of asthma and bronchitis. Ma huang, *Ephedra sinica*, has been used for thousands of years by the Chinese for the same conditions, and is the richest source of ephedrine known.

Another interesting class of natural chemicals are the cardiac glycosides. These chemicals increase the output of blood by the failing heart without an increase in the amount of oxygen required by the heart. This accounts for the use by the medical profession of foxglove, *Digitalis*. However, a number of herbs contain these chemicals and often in a less potentially poisonous form. A modern herbalist would not use digitalis but Lily of the Valley, Hawthorn berries or perhaps Mistletoe.

The Philosophy of Herbalism

The view of herbs as sources of useful chemicals is not that held by modern herbalists. A botanical drug consists of a whole range of chemicals, some in trace quantities and some in large amounts. It must be realised, therefore, that the properties of a herb are not those of an active ingredient but of the whole complex of components. These work together, in many cases counteracting potentially dangerous effects, in other cases reinforcing positive ones. Herbs are clearly a case where the whole is more than the sum of the parts, the properties not being due simply to the individual chemicals present.

Illness in Man is a manifestation of physiological imbalance. Whatever the symptoms, they are but the indicators of a deeper bodily malaise. To treat a 'diseased entity' with specific drugs does at best suppress the manifestation of imbalance. The use of herbs and natural therapeutics provides the practitioner with tools that work at the level of inner balance. The whole of the herb treats the whole body.

Herbalism Today

Modern herbalism has advanced much in its understanding of the disease process since the days of the old herbalists. With this advance in understanding there has developed a different approach to the treatment and management of the ill patient. The therapeutic tools are the same, herbs, but the way they are used has changed.

The person to be treated is viewed as a whole person, not an assortment of symptoms which need fitting into a recognisable syndrome. It is important to recognise that as a physiological whole, all systems and organs are deeply integrated. The functioning of one part of the body affects and conditions the working of all other parts. With this in mind, it becomes clear that any symptoms that appear are the result of a bodily malaise and not simply due to the immediate cause of the symptoms.

When an organ, for example, becomes out of physiological balance for some reason, the manifest symptoms may appear in another organ altogether because of the body's attempts to compensate for the basic malfunction. Thus, a herbalist does not primarily treat symptoms, but attempts to find the deeper cause of the malaise. Of course, herbs will be used to relieve suffering, but in a wider therapeutic framework. Thus, great care is taken to avoid suppressing the manifestation of illness, as this only has the affect of forcing the imbalance deeper and making it more difficult to rectify when the illness surfaces later, as it surely will. It might not be the same symptoms but will undoubtedly have the same basic cause.

The herbalist will, therefore, consider the body of his patient, its history in depth, but also it must be remembered that the psychological state, and indeed the spiritual state must be borne in mind, because the ill patient is a human being and must be treated as such.

In 1864 the National Institute of Medical Herbalists was formed to further the cause of herbalism in this country. It is now a thriving body, the professional body of practising herbalists. It provides an intensive and highly thought-of training course for prospective herbalists. Information on this course and a list of practising herbalists can be obtained from the following addresses:

National Institute of Medical Herbalists,
56 Longbrook Street,
Exeter, EX4 6AH.

The School of Phytotherapy (Herbal Medicine),
Buocksteep Manor, Bodle St. Green,
Nr. Hailsham, E. Sussex, BN27 4RH.

There is also a B.Sc.(Hons.) Degree Course in Herbal Medicine at:

Middlesex University, Queensway,
Enfield, Middlesex, EN3 4SF.

Other useful addresses:

British Herbal Medicine Association,
18 Sussex Square, Brighton, Sussex.

Natural Medicines Society,
Market Chambers, 13a, Market Place, Heanor,
Derby, DE75 7AA.

The Register of Medical Herbalists,
32 King Edward Road, Swansea,
West Glamorgan, SA1 4LL.

Potters (Herbal Supplies) Ltd,
Leyland Mill Lane, Wigan, Lancs. WN1 2SB.
Tel: 01942 234761

are also very helpful and will recommend herbalists in your area.

I am very pleased to have been asked to update the information for the reprint of 'Welsh Herbal Medicine'. I served my 'apprenticeship' with David Hoffmann and during training he was my mentor, teacher and (above all) my friend. I am now the herbalist in the practice he established in 1978 in Cardigan.

Christina Jabroo, Herbalist,
Cardigan Natural Healing Centre,
Manchester House, Grosvenor Hill, Cardigan, SA43 1HY
Tel: 01239 614102.

The Herbal

The herbs described in this book are all herbs which were in common usage by Welsh physicians and householders alike. It was not too long ago that the properties of these common plants were known by most country folk. They are arranged alphabetically using the English names. The Welsh and Latin names are also given. After a brief description of the plant, its habitat and the part used medically, an account of its current medical usage is given. Extracts from the Physicians of Myddfai then follow with page and paragraph numbers from the translation by J. Pughe. Each entry finished with any relevant folk uses or history. An Index to Therapeutic Action can be found on page 78

AGRIMONY : Y Tryw

Agrimonia eupatoria

Agrimony is one of our prettiest wild plants, the erect, round, hairy stem reaching a height of two feet. The numerous pinnate leaves, hairy on both sides, and 5-6 inches long, grow alternately with smaller lanceolate leaflets. The many star-like, small, bright yellow flowers are arranged in long, tapering spikes. It is in flower from July to September.

The actions of agrimony are astringent, diuretic and tonic. It is an old remedy for debility as it gives tone to the whole system. Its mild astringency make it valuable in children's diarrhoea, not least because of its pleasant taste. It is of service for other intestinal conditions such as mucous colitis. It also finds a use in the treatment of grumbling appendicitis. As a diuretic with astringent properties it is of value in urinary incontinance and cystitis. It has been used in cases of dyspepsia and gastro-enteritis but works best when administered in combination with other agents. As a vulnerary it can be used in all cases of bleeding.

FOR INFLAMMATION OF THE MAMMAE
pg. 310*54. Take agrimony, betony and vervain, and pound well, then mix with strong old ale, strain well, and set some milk on the fire; when this boils add the liquor thereto and make a posset thereof, giving it to the woman to drink warm. Let her do this frequently and she will be cured.

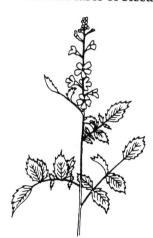

The name agrimony is from Argemone, a word given by the Greek to plants which were healing to the eyes, the name eupatoria refers to Mithridates Eupator, a king who was renowned for his herbal concoctions. A country name for the plant is Aaron's rod, also given to mullein.

BARBERRY : **Y Pren Melyn** *Berberis vulgaris*

The barberry was at one time a common hedgerow plant but is now unusual. This is partly due to its being the host to a rust fungus which attacks wheat and so has been removed by farmers. The stems are woody, growing up to 10 feet tall. It bears small yellow flowers in hanging clusters from April to June, which produce bright red oblong berries which are ripe in August and September. The root and stem bark are used today.

Barberry is primarily a cholagogue, containing an alkaloid which stimulates bile secretion. It finds use in cases of jaundice, inflammation of the gall-bladder and gall-stones. It is a tonic to the spleen. Dilation of the blood vessels is produced with a resulting tendency to a reduction in blood pressure. The root is laxative in moderate dosage. A decoction of the berries or bark is a useful mouthwash and is said to strengthen the gums, relieving pyorrhea. The berries are rich in vitamin C.

'TO CAUSE THE HAIR TO GROW'
pg. 353*318. Take the barberry, and fill an iron pot therewith, fill it up with as much water as it will contain, then boil on a slow fire to the half. With this water, wash your head morning and evening. Take care that the wash does not touch any part where hair should not grow.

The fruits were thought of as a delicacy until quite recently. Mrs Beeton uses them in early editions. The plant also provides quite useful dyes. The leaves give black, the roots give yellow, twigs and young leaves give a red-yellow.

BETONY : **Cribau San Ffraid**   *Betonica officinalis*

Betony, with its characteristic head of dark-lipped flowers, is commonly found on hedgebanks and in grassy places of semi-shade in England, Wales and southern Scotland. It is easily recognised by its four-sided, unbranched stem and long stalked oval basal leaves, with their unusual scalloped edges. The flowers appear from June to August.

It is a plant of wide application, having sedative, astringent, vulnerary, diuretic, carminative and expectorant properties. It is of use in headache, vertigo, anxiety, hysteria and neuralgia. It is also recommended for asthma and bronchitis as well as heartburn. The juice is an excellent wound herb, healing cuts, external ulcers and old sores.

THESE ARE THE VIRTUES OF BETONY
pg. 438*788. He who will habituate himself to drink the juice, will escape the strangury. If it is boiled in white wine, and drank, it will cure the colic, and swelling of the stomach. Pounding it small, expressing the juice and apply it with a feather to the eye of a man, will clear and strengthen his sight, and remove specks from his eye. The juice is a good thing to drop into the ears of those who are deaf.

The powder mixed with honey is useful for those who cough; it will remove the cough and benefit many diseases of the lungs. If boiled with leek seed, it will cure the eye, and brighten as well as strengthen the sight.

Betony was a holy plant, supposedly having many magical properties. It is also used in herbal tobacco.

BLESSED THISTLE : Ysgall Bendigaid

Cnicus benedictus

This is a native of waste stony places in southern Europe which, how-ever, grows well in British gardens. The reddish stem grows to about two feet high and is very branched, scarcely able to keep upright under the weight of its leaves and flowerheads. The leaves are long, narrow, clasping the stem, with prominent pale veins, the irregular teeth of the wavy margin ending in spikes. The flowers are pale yellow. The whole plant is covered in a thin down. The leaves and flowering tops are collected in July, just as the flowers appear.

Blessed thistle is a tonic, stimulant, diaphoretic, emetic and em-menagogue. In large doses it acts as a strong emetic, producing vomiting without pain and inconvenience. Smaller cold infusions are valuable in weak and debilitated conditions of the stomach and as a tonic, creating appetite and preventing sickness. It is now used mainly for nursing mothers, generating an abundant flow of milk.

THE VIRTUES OF THE BLESSED THISTLE
pg. 443*794. The blessed thistle is an aperient; being eaten it will benefit headache, and the midriff also, strength-ening hearing. It strengthens the brain and sight, not only by eating it, but also when the juice is applied to the eye. The herb is also a strengthener of the intellect and memory. It is also good for vertigo, and bleeding from the nose and mouth.

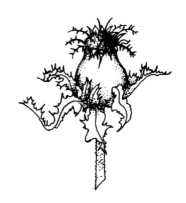

The name Blessed thistle is derived from its properties as a heal-all. Other names include Holy thistle.

BROOM : **Banadle N. Wales**   *Sarothamnus scoparius*
          Banadlen, S. Wales

A native shrub found on heaths, waste ground in woods and hedgerows. It has many branches which bear very small leaves. Large yellow pea-like flowers are borne in May and June, which might cause it to be confused with gorse. However, one touch will show that unlike the rapiers of gorse, broom is thornless. The tops are used.

Broom has been used for many centuries as a medicinal plant, and pharmacology has shown it to be rich in alkaloids which act on the kidneys and heart. It is also a good astringent. As a valuable diuretic it is used in urine retention and dropsy. It gently increases heart output and is used in cases of cardiac dropsy. It can have the effect of inducing labour and so is not used during pregnancy.

FOR SUPPRESSION OF URINE
pg. 313*78. Take broom seed, counting nine and devoting the tenth to God; grind the seed into fine meal and take in drink, or as a confection in boiled honey. If a woman or a maid should do this neither pain or abscess will ever take in her mammae.

As its name implies, the herb is renowned for its useful shape, the ideal natural broom. The Plantagenet kings get their name from the medieval name of broom, Planta Genista. A spray was the badge of Henry II. Broom was a plant of magic and love, as well as medicine, being used by the witches and against them.

BUCKBEAN : Ffa'r Gors   *Menyanthes trifoliata*

Buckbean, or bogbean, grows in spongy bogs, marshes and shallow water throughout Britain. It has a creeping rootstock which is covered by the sheaths of the leaves. These are on long, fleshy petioles and are tripartite, the leaflets being entire and about two inches long and one broad. It blossoms from May to July with very conspicuous flowers borne on up to eighteen inch high stalks.The flowers are outwardly rose coloured and inwardly white and hairy with reddish stamens. A very beautiful plant.

Buckbean is a tonic, cathartic, with deobstruent and febrifuge properties. It finds it's main use in modern herbalism as an ingredient in the treatment of rheumatism, especially when the patient is very weak and run down. It had been used in scurvy and skin diseases in the past. Buckbean tea taken alone or mixed with wormwood, centaury or sage is said to cure dyspepsia and a torpid liver.

ACUTE GASTRODYNIA
pg. 301*2. Take buckbean and powder well. Also burn a quantity of gorse or broom seed in an iron pot, and reduce to a fine powder. Pour a gallon of strong old mead upon the ingredients, then cover it up well and boil, and let it stand covered till cold. You should then drink as much thereof as you may require, night and morning fasting; at other times you should drink nothing but water till you have recovered your health.

BUCKTHORN : **Rhafnwydden** *Rhamnus cathartica*

The purging buckthorn is a deciduous shrub found often as a hedge plant. It may grow to more than 12 feet high, in thickets or along the edge of woods. Its branchlets are usually tipped with sharp spines; and its elliptic, serrated leaves grow in opposite pairs on the stems and branches. During May and June small, green-yellow flowers appear in clusters. The fruit is a black, fleshy, berry-like drupe. It is the fruit that is used medicinally.

The berries of buckthorn are purgative and diuretic. It has been used as a purgative since the ninth century at least.

AN APERIENT DRINK
pg. 316*97. Take the fruit of the buckthorn, express the juice and mix two spoonfuls thereof with a full draught of good ale wort, let the patient drink it, and if it does not act let him drink another draught without the buckthorn. When it has acted let him take for food some warm oatmeal gruel made from spring water, mixing therewith some honey, butter, and unsifted wheaten bread, let this be done three times in nine days and it will purge the body of all corrupt humors; after this course let him live for nine days further on milk food and wheaten bread with the bran retained, alternately with warm water and flour before mentioned.

Apart from being a rather drastic cure for constipation, the purging buckthorn gives a beautiful colour used for dyeing and in the making of pigments. Unripe dried berries, dried, powdered and boiled with alum gives a saffron which was much used in the 17th century for tinting leather.

BURDOCK : **Y Cyngaw**   *Arctium lappa*

A large biennial plant growing up to 4 feet tall with large heart-shaped leaves, purple flowers and bristly burrs. The flowers appear in loose clusters from July to September. The leaves are gathered in July as are the roots of the first year plants.

Burdock is an alterative, chologogue, diuretic and diaphoretic. Its main use is found in the treatment of scaly skin diseases such as eczema and psoriasis, where it combines well with yellow dock and red clover. It is also of value in rheumatic conditions. The high content of mucilage gives it demulcent properties which are of use in stomach ailments. The leaves are used externally as a poultice in tumours and gouty swellings. A fomentation of the decoction is used in skin diseases.

SQUAMOUS ERUPTION
(psoriasis)
pg. 420*702. Take the leaves of burdock, pound them well with a little wine and strain. Take three spoonfuls, night, morning and noon, and let a decoction of burdock be your only drink. The part should be fomented with the decoction also, as hot as you can bear it, and anoint it afterwards with an unguent composed of wine, olive oil and honey. Proven.

The name of his herb comes in part from the expanded flower head, the burr.

> Rosalind: How full of briers is this working-day world.
> Celia: They are but burrs, cousin, thrown upon thee in holiday foolery. If we walk not in the trodden paths, our very petticoats will catch them.

CENTAURY : **Ysgol Fair** *Erythraea centaurium*

Centaury is a beautiful little plant of dry pastures. The stems grow up to one foot high, with opposite leaves which are lanceolate-ovate. These leaves have three to four longitudinal ribs, entire margins and smooth. The plant flowers in July and August to produce red-pink blooms and characteristic twisted anthers. The whole plant is used in medicine and is very bitter.

This herb is aromatic, stomachic and a bitter tonic. It stimulates the activity of the salivary, stomach and intestinal glands, thereby relieving constipation and gas and promoting proper digestion. This activity probably accounts for many of its other beneficial effects. The tea is commonly used for heartburn, colic, suppressed menstruation and anaemia. It is particularly recommended for people who lead a sedentary life and who don't get much outdoor exercise.

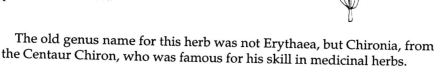

FOR PAIN IN THE CARDIAC REGION
pg. 323*129. Take the centaury, boil well in old ale, then remove the herbs from the ale, and pound well in a mortar, boil again well, and express through a fine cloth, take this juice mixed with twice the quantity of honey, boil moderately and habituate yourself to take it, fasting for nine days, and through the help of God it will heal the oppression and pain about the heart.

The old genus name for this herb was not Erythaea, but Chironia, from the Centaur Chiron, who was famous for his skill in medicinal herbs.

CHICKWEED :
A Gwlydd y Dom, Llysau'r Dom

Stellaria media

Chickweed is a very common plant of waste places, roadsides and gardens. The plant has a usually creeping, brittle stem from 4 to 12 inches long. The small white flowers, with deeply cleft petals, can be found all year round.

It is demulcent, expectorant, laxative and anti-rheumatic. Internally it is useful in constipation, although it is more often used in inflammatory conditions of the respiratory organs and interal membranes generally. Its greatest use is externally where it allays itching and soothes inflamed and irritated areas. An ointment of chickweed, often with marshmallow root or slippery elm, is indicated in eczema, psoriasis and indolent ulcers. A poultice is used for carbuncles and abscesses.

A PLASTER TO REDUCE A SWELLING
RESULTING FROM AN ACCIDENT
pg. 343*260. Take mallows, chamomile, maiden hair, chickweed and ground ivy, boil them well in the stalest urine you can get. Apply to the affected part as a plaster, and it will reduce the swelling.

The genus name Stellaria is the old medieval name describing the star-like flowers. It is unfortunate that so many garderners do not know the virtues of this very common weed. Tons are incinerated annually, a great waste. Mabey gives the following recipe, an excellent one:

> Strip bunches of the whole plant and wash well. Put into a saucepan with no extra water, add a knob of butter, seasoning and some chopped spring onions. Simmer gently for about ten minutes, turning all the time. Finish off with a dash of lemon juice or a sprinkling of grated nutmeg.

CLEAVERS : **Gwlydd y Perthi** *Galium aparine*

Cleavers, or goosegrass, is a member of the bedstraw family, a native British herb. It is found scrambling over hedgerows throughout the country by means of tiny, down-curved bristles on its stems and leaves, which are in whorls of six or more. It has small lanceolate leaves also in whorls of six to nine. The flowers are tiny and white with the petals arranged like a Maltese cross. The small fruits are also covered in the small hooks and tenaciously cling to anything they touch, hence the name.

Cleavers is a diuretic and alterative. It is used in painful or scanty urine, cystitis, etc. As an alterative it is used for skin diseases such as psoriasis, and is considered a specific for inflammation of the Lymph glands, adenitis.

THE VIRTUES OF CLEAVERS
pg. 444*795. The juice taken in spring and summer as the only drink will expel and completely destroy eruptive poison from the blood. This virus is the cause of all eruptions, boils, scalds, scrophula, lepra, cancer, erysipelas, pneumonia, dropsy, rheumatism, gout, strangury, all sorts of fevers, pocks of flesh and skin, all watery diseases of the eye, all phlegm of the head or stomach, all white swellings of the joints, every inflamed condition of the blood, every headache attended with fever, for there is hardly a disease affecting the human body, but that it is occasioned by an eruptive poison in the blood.

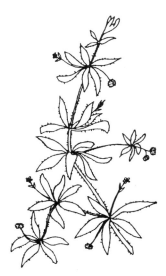

The juice is thus obtained. Take the whole herb and pound well; then put in an unglazed earthenware vessel, and fill it up without pressing them; then pour on as much as it will admit of pure spring water, and let it stand a night.

COLTSFOOT :
Troed yr Ebol, Pesychlys

Tussilago farfara

The creeping rootstock of this plant sends up a flowering stem in February which is downy white and scaly, crowned with a single composite yellow flower. The leaves appear after the flowering stem has died down. The shape of the leaves gives the plant its name. The under surface of the leaves are downy white. The leaves are collected in June and early July, the flower stalks in February and March.

The genus name, Tussilago, means 'cough dispeller' and shows the renown of this herb as an expectorant remedy. It is also demulcent and anti-catarrhal. Thus we find it used in all coughs, whooping cough, bronchitis, pleurisy, laryngitis, asthma, etc. The dried leaves have long been smoked to relieve chronic bronchitis, shortness of breath (dyspnoea) and dry coughs. The crushed leaves are applied externally for insect bites, swellings, burns, inflammations, etc. It combines well with hyssop, mullein and horehound.

FOR PAIN IN THE LEGS
pg. 370*418. Take the herb called Coltsfoot (they are like burdock in appearance), boil them well in the milk of a cow of one colour with oaten groats and May butter, and apply warm to the painful part.

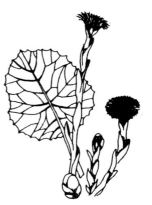

COMFREY : **Cwmffri**   *Symphytum officinalis*

Comfrey is a large, impressive plant found in damp fields, waste places, ditch and river sides. The hairy stem is two to three feet high, freely branched, rough and angular. Egg-shaped to lanceolate leaves, with wavy edges, hug the stem above, the lower ones having long stalks, they are all large and hairy. The plant produces yellowish, bluish or purplish-white flowers in May and June, all on one side of the stem. The root and rhizome or leaves are used.

The country name 'knitbone' well describes one of the actions of comfrey, it is a vulnerary of great renown. No house should be without comfrey ointment. There is a clear pharmacological basis to this. The plant is the richest source of a chemical called allantoin, which has the property of stimulating cell division, so that where there has been a cut, the two sides are stimulated to proliferate new cells. Thus the healing process is greatly speeded up.

The herb is used for all wounds, burns, etc., as an ointment or any other root preparation. It also has demulcent actions which in combination with the healing effects make it of great service in the treatment of peptic ulceration of any kind. Similarly for any inflammation of the alimentary canal such as colitis. It is also a pectoral herb of note, being used in coughs and bronchitis. Externally it is specific for chronic varicose ulcers. For gastric use it is often mixed with marshmallow and meadowsweet.

Comfrey has long been renowned for its curative properties, the name Symphytum being derived from the Greek name given to it by Dioscorides, meaning 'grow-together plant'. Gerard gives a long list of virtues, some of which are rather unexpected: "The slimie substance of the root made in a posset of ale, and given to drinke against the paine in the back, gotten by any violent motion, as wrestling, or over much use of women, does in fower or five daies perfectly cure the same, although the involuntary flowing of the seed in men be gotten therby."

COWSLIP : **Briallu Mair**   *Primula veris*

Cowslip has a round downy stem rising well above the leaves, which lie rosette-like on the ground. The leaves grow from the root, stalkless, undivided, with a velvety appearance similar to primrose leaves, but shorter and rounder. It bears yellow tubular flowers bunched together on one stalk, each flower emerging from the same point, outer blossoms drooping. It is a plant of moist pastures and open places. At one time a common plant, it is now regrettably becoming rare due to the draining of its habitat and the over-collection by flower lovers.

Cowslip has sedative and antispasmodic properties. It is indicated where the reduction of involuntary spasmodic movements, restlessness and similar symptoms is called for. It is an excellent mild sedative useful in insomnia. It is generally applicable for strengthening the nerves and brain.

FOR THE BITE OF A MAD DOG
pg. 337*218. Seek some cowslips, pound them, mix with milk, and administer to the patient as his only drink for nine days, being first strained through a fine cloth; others boil the cowslips with the sweet milk, straining them under a press, and administering as a drink to the patient, for nine days. The patient should drink as much as he can there-of abstaining from all other aliment for the time.

The name cowslip is the polite form of the rather unfortunate name of cowplop. The plant has also been called Herb Peter and Key Flower, due to the flower's resemblance to a bunch of keys.

Cowslip wine is perhaps one of the best country wines, with a delicate flavour and beautiful, pale yellow colour. The number of flower heads needed to make this drink are probably a major cause of its decline in the wild.

DANDELION : **Dant y Llew** *Taraxacum officinalis*

The stem of this almost ubiquitous plant is slender, hollow, and contains the familiar milk-like juice. The long thin leaves, which are broader towards the top than at the base, are toothedged in a slightly backward direction. Each of the petals, of which only the central portion of the yellow flower is wholly composed, are strap-like in form. The roots are long dark brown, and bitter to the taste, although not unpleasantly so. The roots are the part usually used, although the leaves are also of service.

Dandelion is a most excellent diuretic, laxative and cholagogue. It is generally a stimulant to the system, but especially to the urinary organs, and is chiefly used in kidney and liver disorders. Modern herbalists use this herb in inflammation of the gall-balder, gall-stones and jaundice. As a diuretic it is found in most mixtures prescribed for kidney and bladder problems. It is considered a specific in cases of atonic dyspepsia with constipation. It is also relevant in the treatment of rheumatism.

FOR JAUNDICE
pg. 432*753. Take dandelion, corn blue bottle, and garden parsley; pound them well with a good strong ale, and keep it carefully in a narrow mouthed water bottle. Let it be used the first thing in the morning an hour before food, and the last thing at night after food. The dose should be from four egg shellfuls to a pint.

The leaves and root of dandelion have culinary as well as medicinal uses. The young leaves make a delicious addition to spring salads and also as the fillings for sandwiches. The dried and powdered root makes an excellent coffee substitute.

ELECAMPANE :
Marchalan y Llwyglas

Inula helenium

A striking handsome plant growing from 4 to 5 feet high. The whole plant is downy with a rosette of leaves which are from 1 to 1½ feet long and 4 inches wide in the middle. It is in flower in July and August with large, bright yellow flowers. It is an introduced herb, widely scattered though uncommon in fields, wayside, copse, etc. The root and the rhizome are used medicinally.

Elecampane was used primarily as a pulmonary herb in bronchitis, asthma, tuberculosis, etc., giving relief to respiratory difficulties and assisting expectoration. It is useful in whooping cough, acute bronchial catarrh and especially children's coughs. Research has shown that the bitter principle helenin, present in elecampane, is a powerful bacteriocide and antiseptic. Another use of the root is as an alterative in skin diseases, where it is used internally and externally. It is also diuretic and diaphoretic.

FOR COUGH AND DYSPNOEA
pg. 358*338. Take the root of elecampane, two pennyworth of black pepper, and the same of the roots of mallows. Let them be powdered and made into a confection with clarified honey. Take as much as a pigeon's egg the first thing in the morning and the last at night. It is proven.

'TO STRENGTHEN THE TEETH AND MAKE THEM WHITE'
pg. 334*261. Take elecampane and scrub your teeth therewith briskly, it will make them firm, white and healthy.

The herb was known to the ancients as a medicine and condiment. Gerard tells us: "it took its name Helenium of Helena, wife of Menelaus, who had her hands full of it when Paris stole her away to Troy."

ELDER FLOWER :
Blodau yr Ysgawen

Sambucus nigra

This familiar small tree, 12 to 20 feet high, has young branches containing light, spongy pith, with a bark that is light grey and corky externally. The leaves are opposite, deep green and smooth. Creamy-white, flat-topped masses of flowers bloom in July, to be followed by the decorative drooping bunches of purplish-black, juicy berries.

The flowers of this tree are strongly diaphoretic and anticatarrhal. They form part of the most famous herbal tea, elder flower and peppermint tea, which is renowned as a cold and 'flu tea. The mixture is greatly improved by the addition of yarrow. It also has a role to play in the treatment of chronic nasal catarrh associated with deafness due to mucus. It is similarly used in sinusitis.

FOR INFLAMMATION OF THE LUNGS
pg. 397*571. Take elder flowers, or the leaves, or the green inner bark, and wood sorrel; boil in the whey of goat or kine's milk, and let it be your only drink for nine weeks. So that you may not be in want of the flowers, let them be gathered in their season and dried in the sun. Keep them and boil them in the whey as required. This is useful for all sorts of fevers in the blood and humours.

Elder is a tree of great magical involvement. The wood was considered to be very unlucky indeed and no forester would cut or use it. One old legend is that if you burn elder wood on your fire you would see the devil sitting on the chimney. Another legend is that Judas hanged himself upon an Elder, in token of which the ear of Judas, 'Jew's Ear', the fungus *Hurneola auricula Judae*, grows from the bark.

EYEBRIGHT :
Golwg Crist, Llygad Crist

Euphrasis officinalis agg

This genus of herbs contains many different species, most of which hybridise with each other causing much variation within the general pattern. They are small plants from 2 to 8 inches high with deeply cut leaves and small, white or purplish-lipped flowers with a yellow eye. It is found on commons, heaths and in meadows. The whole plant, including the root, is gathered between July and September whilst in bloom.

Eyebright is the eye remedy par excellence, being used in all eye ailments such as weakness of the eye, ophthalmia and conjunctivitis. As an eye lotion it can be combined with witchhazel to great effect. It has anti-catarrhal properties which explain its use in nasal catarrh and sinusitis. It is also astringent.

TO STRENGTHEN THE SIGHT
pg. 307*39. Take eyebright and red fennel, a handful of each and half a handful of rue, distil, and wash your eye daily therewith.

Its fame as an eye tonic is shown in 'Paradise Lost' where the Archangel anoints Adam's eyes with Euphrasia and Rue and three drops from the well of life, until he could see death and the miserable future of mankind.

The Welsh name 'Golwg Crist' means Christ Sight and 'Llygad Crist' means Christ's Eye.

FENNEL : Ffunel   *Foeniculum dulce*

Fennel is a large, handsome, umbelliferous plant found on cliffs, heaths and grown in gardens. The erect stems grow to about four feet, striated, smooth and freely branching. The leaves are very finely cut. It flowers in mid-summer to give umbels of golden yellow blooms. It has a characteristic sweet and aromatic smell. The seeds are used.

Fennel is antispasmodic, carminative, diuretic, expectorant, galactogogue and stimulant. Both seeds and roots are excellent stomach remedies. It helps to arouse appetite, relieve colic, abdominal cramps and flatulance. The oil is useful in gargles for coughing and hoarseness. If the seeds are boiled in barley water, they are said to promote the flow of milk in nursing mothers.

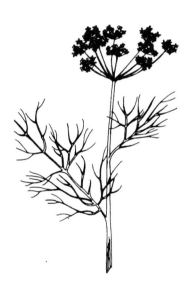

THE VIRTUES OF THE FENNEL
pg. 439*790. The fennel is warm and dry in the second degree and is useful for diseases of the eye. It is good for every kind of poison in a man's body, being drank in the form of powder mixed with white wine or strong old mead. It is useful for tertian ague and inflammatory fever; and if the seed or herb is boiled in water, till it is strong of the virtues of the herb, and the head, when subject to the headache, washed therewith, it will greatly benefit and cure the same, when the headache is occasioned by cold or fever. It will remove the headache very quickly.

Fennel was known to the ancients and was cultivated by the Romans for its aromatic fruits and succulent edible shoots. Pliny had much faith in its medicinal properties, according no less than twenty-two remedies to it.

FEVERFEW :
Feddygen Fenyw

Chrysanthemum parthenium

Feverfew is a common member of the compositae (daisy) family. It is found growing on hedgerows throughout the country. The round, leafy, branching stem bears alternate, bipinnate leaves. The flowers appear in June and July and have yellow discs, and from ten to twenty white, toothed rays.

Feverfew has emmenagogue, carminative, aperient and bitter properties. It is used in hysterical complaints, nervousness, low spirits and as a general tonic. In America it has been used in alcoholic D.T.s. It is useful in colic and flatulence. As an emmenagogue it eases difficulties with menstruation. Externally a warm infusion eases bites and stings from insects.

A HEALING OINTMENT FOR BRUISES
pg. 337*213. Take feverfew, ribwort plantain, garden sage, and bugle, equal parts of each, pound them well and boil in unsalted May butter, then express through a fine linen, and keep in a box. Anoint the disease therewith and it will cure it. If there be dead flesh therein, take some sloes, or sulphate of copper, or red precipitate of mercury in powder, and mix with some of the ointment, then it will destroy the dead flesh, and promote the healing of the sore.

The name feverfew is a corruption from the word febrifuge, a description of its tonic and fever dispelling properties. Gardeners have used feverfew to attract toads to their gardens, the best natural cure for snails and slugs. The plant is often found around old houses or the sites of old houses as it was planted to purify the air and ward off disease.

GARLIC : **Garlec**

Allium sativum

Garlic is a perennial plant that is widely cultivated as one of the most common kitchen herbs. The garlic bulb is compound, consisting of individual cloves enclosed together in a white skin. The stem is simple and entire, enclosed at the bottom by the leaf sheaths. The stem is topped by a rounded umbel of small, white flowers.

Garlic is a most potent medicinal plant. Its actions include those of a diaphoretic, expectorant, antiseptic, bacteriostatic, antiviral, hypotensive and anthelmintic. In all respiratory problems it is especially indicated. Thus it plays a role in the treatment of chronic and acute bronchitis, respiratory catarrh, recurrent colds, whooping-cough, bronchitic asthma, etc. In all cases of infection due to bacteria and viruses it is of great service. In the first world war the juice was used in cases of supporating wounds, applied on swabs of sterile sphagnum moss. It can be applied externally for all infected sores or wounds.

FOR NOISE IN THE HEAD, PREVENTING HEARING

pg. 338*223. Take a clove of garlic, prick in three or four places in the middle, dip in honey and insert in the ear, covering it with some black wool. Let the patient sleep on the other side every night leaving the clove in the ear for seven or eight nights unchanged. It will prevent the running of the nose and restore the hearing.

Garlic was a herb of magic as well as medicine, being thought to possess magical power against evil, and thus it was used in many charms and counter charms.

GREATER CELANDINE : Melynllys

Chelidonium majus

This herb is not to be confused with the similarly named Lesser Celandine. It is a relative of the Poppy, with the typical four wrinkled petals of that family, yellow in this case. The slender stem reaches to between 1½ and 3 feet high and is much branched. The leaves are a fresh green colour with deep divisions to the central rib. The whole plant is rich in an orange latex which contains abundant alkaloids. It is found chiefly near habitations on banks, hedgerows and walls.

Celandine is an ancient herb, mentioned by Dioscorides and has a long history as a wart cure, the highly irritant latex being applied direct. A similar use was found in the treatment of corns. However, if the latex touched healthy skin it produced inflammation and blistering. Celandiene was also used as a soothing herb for sore eyes and the removal of spots on the cornea. In modern herbalism the herb is used as a purgative, cholagogue, diuretic and especially in the treatment of the gall-bladder. It is considered a specific in the treatment of gall-stones. It combines well with Dandelion.

A GOOD EYE SALVE
pg. 398*580. Take vinegar, white wine, the juice of celandine, and plantain, mix them together in a pan, cover over and let them stand therein 3 days and 3 nights, take it hence, keep it in a box and anoint thine eye therewith.

Dioscorides tells us that the name Chelidonion, a swallow in Greek, was given to the herb as it flowers on the swallows' return in the spring.

GROUND IVY :
Llysiau'r Gerwyn

Glechoma hederacea

Ground ivy is one of our commonest plants, flourishing upon sunny hedgebanks and waste ground in all parts of Great Britain. It is a relative of the mint, but with a less pleasant smell. Growing up to 10 inches, it has bright purple two-lipped flowers growing in whorls, blossoming from April onwards. The leaves resemble those of ivy in shape and grow from the four-sided stem. The aerial parts are gathered during spring and early summer whilst still in bloom.

This herb has a long history of medicinal use both of medical men and housewives. It is expectorant, diuretic, astringent and mildly stimulant. Use is made of it in kidney diseases and indigestion, but primarily in chest complaints, being of value in coughs, bronchitis, etc. It was at one time sold in the streets of London as a blood purifier, being made into a wholesome drink which cleared the lungs.

FOR WHOOPING COUGH AND BRONCHITIS
pg. 381*499. Take ground ivy in milk and water, and administer to the patient every morning fasting, and in the evening. It will cure him.

The value of this herb is greatly increased due to its use in brewing. Thus we find another name for ground ivy is alehoof.

HOREHOUND (WHITE) :
Llwyd y Cŵn

Marribium vulgare

Horehound grows to a height of up to two feet tall. The four-cornered stem sends out spreading branches covered with white, woolly hair. The leaves, also covered in the same soft hair, are egg-shaped and deeply toothed. The small white flowers appear during July in dense whorls above the upper leaves.

White horehound is perhaps one of the best known chest remedies. It is very effective in all coughs, colds and pulmonary complaints. It is expectorant and antispasmodic. It is used in acute and chronic bronchitis, and is considered a specific in bronchitis with a non-productive cough. It is also used in whooping cough. It may be combined with rue, liquorice root and marshmallow root to give an excellent and delicious cough remedy. For children's coughs and croup, it is best given as a syrup.

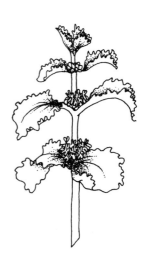

A MEDICINE FOR PNEUMONIA
pg. 321*122. Take the white horehound, and pound well, then add some pure water thereto, letting it stand for three hours, then strain through a fine cloth, add a good deal of honey to the strained liquor, and put on a low fire to warm; take half a draught thereof every three hours, and let your diet be the best wheaten bread and milk; when thirsty, take an apple, and cover it with good old cider, eat the apple, in an hour drink the cider, and let this be your only diet.

White horehound was at one time the main ingredient of cough candy.

HYSSOP : **Isob**

Hyssopus officinalis

Hyssop is a bushy, evergreen plant which was introduced into this country from southern Europe where it is indigenous. The plant consists of several square, branched downy stems which are woody at the bottom. It bears opposite linear leaves and whorls of flowers, each containing six to fifteen flowers, up the tops of the branches. The colour of the flowers varies from rose to bluish-purple and they appear from June to October.

The actions of hyssop are expectorant, diaphoretic, carminative, sedative. It is of great value in all coughs and colds. It is used in bronchitis and chronic nasal catarrh, where it may well be combined with horehound. As a pleasant tasting tea, it may be used in all chest problems. Its diaphoretic nature makes it valuable in feverish colds, etc. As a sedative it has been used in hysteria and petit mal. Combined with the flowers of marigold it is used for mild skin rashes in children.

FOR TIGHTNESS OF THE CHEST
pg. 370*419. Take hyssop and centaury in equal portions, pound well and strain carefully, mix white of eggs with the strained juice, and drink for three days fasting.

Hyssop is a name of Greek origin. The Hyssop of Dioscorides was named azob, a holy herb, because it was used for cleaning holy places. It is alluded to in the Bible: 'Purge me with Hyssop, and I shall be clean'.

MISTLETOE : **Uchelwydd**   *Viscum album*

The mistletoe is an evergreen, semi-parasitic plant, which is found on the branches of deciduous trees. Its most famous host is the oak, on which it is rarely found, it more commonly being seen on apple trees, lime and hawthorn. Roots growing from the yellow-green, forked stem penetrate through the bark into the wood of the tree, its host. The leaves are opposite, leathery, yellow-green and narrow. Pale yellow or green flowers appear from March to May, the females developing into sticky white berries which ripen from September to November.

Mistletoe is a nervine, antispasmodic with hypotensive properties. That means that it lowers blood pressure, and acts as a cardiac depressant. It is used, therefore, in the treatment of high blood pressure, arteriosclerosis, and a number of heart problems. It is particularly good in headaches associated with high blood pressure. As a nervine it finds use in hysteria, epilepsy, chorea and other diseases of the nervous system.

In any case of bodily debility, whether in the nerves, joints, back, head or brain, stomach, heart, lungs or kidneys, take three spoonfuls of the decoction, and mix with boiling water, ale, mead or milk.

It will promote fruitfulness, the begetting of children and restrain seminal flux. The man who takes a spoonful thereof daily in his drink will enjoy uninterrupted health, strength of body and manly vigour.

The best places to procure it are Monmouthshire, Somersetshire, Brechnockshire and Shropshire.

MALLOW : **Malws** *Malva sylvestris*

The common, or blue, mallow is a robust plant 3 or 4 feet high, growing at the edge of fields and old meadows. Its stem is round, thick and strong, the leaves stalked, five to seven lobed, downy with prominent veins on the undersurface. The flowers are showy, bright mauve-purple with dark veins. When they first expand in June, the plant is handsome, but as the summer advances, the leaves lose their deep green colour and the stems assume a ragged appearance.

Common mallow is little used today as it has been superseded by marsh mallow, a plant richer in mucilage and generally more efficacious. It is astringent, demulcent and expectorant. It makes a good soothing tea for coughs, hoarseness, bronchitis, any inflammation of the throat and irritation of the respiratory passages. It is useful wherever a demulcent is called for. Externally a decoction can be used as a wash for wounds and sores.

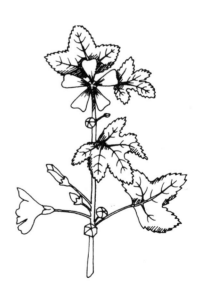

FOR INFLAMMATORY WOUNDS, WHEREBY THE PATIENT IS PRE-VENTED FROM SLEEPING
pg. 318*110. Take holly bark, mallow, the middle bark of the elder, equal quantities of each, and add thereto lard and wine in the same proportions; boil well until it becomes thick, then take a cloth and spread some warm on a tent also; insert this in the wound, and cover it over with the anointed cloth; apply some powdery unguent on the wound with the tent, and by the help of God it will be healed.

MARIGOLD :
Swyn-ystres, Melyn Mair

Celendula officinalis

Whilst not a native of Britain, marigold is a commonly grown garden flower. It is an annual plant with an angular, branched, hairy stem, growing from 1 to 2 feet high. The leaves are alternate, without stalks, and with widely spaced teeth. It bears golden orange flowers of the daisy type. The flower heads are the part usually used although the leaf has its uses.

Marigold is a diaphoretic, antispasmodic, vulnerary, antiseptic, anit-inflammatory and emmenagogue. It is used in cases of ulcers, internal ones such as duodenal ulcers, and external ones. As an emmenagogue it is used in suppressed and painful periods. It has been widely used for all feverish conditions, especially in children. Externally it can be used in various forms as an application for cuts, burns and any inflammation of the skin. As a wash with witch hazel it is found to be very useful in the treatment of varicose veins.

FOR TYPHUS FEVER
pg. 418*692. Take marigold, pound well with good wine, vinegar, strong mead, or strong ale. Strain carefully, and drink a good draught in the morning fasting, whilst the pestilence lasts. If your are taken ill, you will need no other than this as your only drink. It is a good preservative against the foreign pestilence called the plague.

Marigold flowers have long been used as a cosmetic aid. They will tone up the skin, and as already pointed out, are antiseptic. The essential oil can be added to cold creams, and the infusion has been used as a hair colour.

MARSHMALLOW :
Malws Bendigaid

Althaea officinalis

This erect plant grows to a height of three feet on marshes near the sea. It can be distinguished from the common mallow by the velvety down covering the stems and leaves. The leaves are three to five lobed. The flowers, pink in colour, appear in large panicles between July and September. The roots are thick and fleshy, resembling those of parsnips. The roots and leaves are used medicinally.

Marshmallow is a first-rate demulcent, with diuretic, expectorant and vulnerary properties. It is indicated in most respiratory conditions, especially bronchitis where there is much catarrh. It is also useful in irritating coughs and colds. The leaf is most appropriate in chest conditions. The root is most appropriate in intestine inflammations and especially gastric or duodenal ulcers. Its diuretic and demulcent properties adapt it to urinary complaints and, as there is no astringent action, it is particularly suitable in the treatment of nephritis, cystitis and gravel. It may be used externally as an ointment or poultice in skin inflammations.

TO EASE HEAT AND PAIN IN WOUNDS
pg. 433*764. Take the roots of marshmallows, and the middle bark of elder, equal parts of each, add thereto an equal quantity of white wine, and boil well till it becomes thick; then spread this on a well-stretched linen cloth as a poultice. If the wound closes prematurely, get the herb called bryony, make it into a plaster, apply thereto, and it will open it.

The derivation of the genus name Althaea is from the Greek altho, to cure. Its healing properties were well-known by the ancients. As with many medicinal plants, it has also been used as a food source.

MUGWORT :
Y Ganwraidd Lwydd

Artemisia vulgaris

Mugwort abounds on hedgebanks and waysides throughout the British Isles. It is a tall plant growing up to 4 feet tall, with highly divided leaves, dark green on the upper surface and silvery white beneath. The flowers, which are dull yellow or purplish clusters, bloom in July and August. The leaves and stems are gathered in August whilst the roots are dug in the Autumn, washed and dried.

This herb is a stimulating bitter tonic with nervine, emmenagogue, diuretic, diaphoretic and vermifuge properties. Its chief use is as an emmenagogue to regulate menstruation, often combined with penny-royal and southernwood. The bitter properties are an aid to digestion whilst its diaphoretic properties are useful at the onset of a cold. As a nervine, mugwort was a popular remedy for palsy and epilepsy. It was also used for hysteria, but perhaps of greatest renown was its use as a reliever of the weariness of travel.

FOR HYSTERIA
pg. 370*421. Take mugwort, red fennel and red mint, boil well in old ale, and strain care-fully through a cloth; drink it warm and you will recover.

Mugwort is a powerfully magic herb, known throughout Europe in the Middle Ages as Mater Herbarum, Mother of Herbs. It had the power to ward off evil spirits and ghosts and was hung in Welsh houses for this purpose at least to the 16th century.

NETTLE : **Ddynhaden** *Urtica dioica*

This plant is a native British herb, and surely needs no description, for as Keble Martin says in his Flora, it is perhaps too common. It is renowned for its sting which every child knows can be cured by rubbing with dock leaves. It is a strange fact that the juice of nettles themselves is an antidote to the sting!

The plant is astringent, diuretic and galactogogue, haemostatic and tonic. The fresh juice or an infusion stimulates the digestion and promotes the flow of milk. It is used in cases of haemorrhage, especially uterine. For nervous eczema, especially in children, it is considered specific. A decoction is good for diarrhoea. It has found much use in the care of hair and is a constituent of many herbal shampoos.

THE FOLLOWING ARE THE VIRTUES OF THE NETTLE

pg. 438*787. Take the juice of this herb mixed with white wine, strain carefully, and let it cool. Drink some thereof night and morning; it will cure you of the jaundice, renovate the blood, and remove any disease existing therein. If the juice is taken, mixed half and half with barley wort, it will cure the pleurisy of the side, and will renovate and invigorate an aged man in body and mind.

The nettle has many uses other than medicinal. It makes an excellent vegetable in the spring, boiled and well seasoned with herbs, garlic, etc., finally garnished with butter. The young shoots or just the small upper leaves only should be used.

Another use is as a source of fibre. It produces a strong smooth fibre, much used at one time for rope and cloth making.

PARSLEY : **Perllys**   *Petroselinum crispum*

Parsley is a biennial or perennial herb which is found in cultivation everywhere. The leaves are deeply cleft and are shiny and dark green. The white or greenish-yellow flowers appear in umbels from July to August. The aerial parts and seeds are used in medicine.

The uses of parsley are many and are by no means restricted to cooking. The most familiar use of the leaves is as flavouring in soups and other dishes. In medicine the two-year-old roots are employed, also the leaves, and the seeds for the extraction of the oil. The herb is strongly diuretic, carminative and tonic. It is used in urine retention, kidney stone and jaundice. The oil is a safe emmenagogue.

THE FOLLOWING ARE THE VIRTUES OF PARSLEY

pg. 439*789. The parsley is a good herb of a warm hot nature, and moist in the third degree. It is useful in all foods as a generator of blood. It will remove obstruction of the veins and arteries in a man's body, so that the humours may circulate properly as they should. This it will certainly do.

It is well to employ parsley for the relief of fainting, tertian ague, pleurisy and dropsy, the juice being taken for three days successively without any other drink. It will stimulate the spirits greatly, and strengthen the stomach.

PLANTAIN : **Llydan y Ffordd**   *Plantago major*

The great plantain is a native British herb with a characteristic basal rosette of large, ovate leaves. It bears very small, brownish-purple flowers growing close together on a spike about five inches high. It is a very common plant growing in meadows, waste place, edges of fields, etc.

Plantain is considered to be a diuretic, alterative and astringent. Thus we find it used in cases of diarrhoea and piles, often combined with other herbs. For piles it is used internally and externally as an ointment. It is specific for piles when they are bleeding and there is much irritation. It would be appropriate in cases of cystitis where this is accompanied by blood in the urine. It may also be used in respiratory conditions such as coughs and hoarseness. The expressed juice is excellent for chronic catarrh. A wash is of value for skin conditions such as ringworm, and may be used as a douche in leucorrhea.

A LOTION TO WASH AN INFLAMED PART
pg. 303*15. Take the greater plantain, honey-suckle, and white roses, distil together, and in the product put some camphor, and let it remain in this water constantly.

Plantago gets its name from the Latin planta, sole of the foot. This refers to the shape of the leaf. In both North America and New Zealand it is called Englishman's foot, as it seemed to sprout up where ever he set his foot.

REDSAGE : **Geidwad** *Salvia officinalis*

Sage is not a native herb of these islands, it having been imported from southern Europe many centuries ago. The stem and leaves are reddish, the whole plant growing to about 12 inches all. The stem is four-sided and wiry. The leaves are opposite each other, with strongly marked veins, about 1½ ins. long. The flowers are in whorls, purplish and the corollas lipped. They blossom in August. The whole plant is highly aromatic due to the volatile oils present.

It is stimulant astringent, tonic and carminative in action. Its most common use today is for the treatment of various mouth conditions. The infusion is used as a wash for mouth ulcers, and as a gargle in inflamed sore throats, being excellent for relaxed throat and tonsils, also for ulcerated throat. The gargle is useful for bleeding gums and to prevent an excessive flow of saliva.

THE VIRTUES OF SAGE

pg. 437*785. They are useful when boiled to strengthen the nerves. If an infusion sweetened with honey is drank, it is useful for the lungs. If the foetus in utero is dead, let the woman boil sage with white wine, strain it carefully, and she will be delivered of the same with safety to her life. Also pound this herb, apply to a poisoned wound, and it will extract the poison; though the wound be full of corruption, it will be cleansed to the very bottom.

It is a good thing for those in health to drink half a draught in the morning fasting of this potion, in order to preserve health and prolong life.

ROSEMARY :
Ysbwynwydd, Rhosmari

Rosmarinus officinalis

The evergreen leaves of this shrubby herb are about 1 inch long, linear, with down-curved edges, dark green above and paler below. They have a very distinctive aroma. The flowers are small and pale blue.

Rosemary is tonic, astringent, diaphoretic and stimulant. Oil of rosemary has the carminative properties of other volatile oils and is an excellent stomachic and nervine, curing many cases of headache.

Rosemary was a highly thought of plant, used extensively by the Physicians, two and half pages being dedicated to its virtues.

THE FOLLOWING ARE THE VIRTUES
OF ROSEMARY

pg. 440*791. Take the flowers, mix with honey, and eat them daily fasting. You will not suffer from nausea or other noxious condition. It will reomove the colic for three hours. Take also the leaves of rosemary and woodsage; making them into a potion and adding honey. It is an excellent remedy for the stranguary, stone and catarrh.

Also, put their flowers or leaves under your head in bed, and you will not be troubled with disagreeable dreams, or oppressed with anxiety of the mind. Also if your carry a stick or fragment of this shrub, no evil spirit can come near you, or anyone do you any harm.

It is useful as a lotion for the head when affected with a headache from cold or fever, or when a man is threatened with insanity.

By washing each morning with the decoction and allowing it to dry naturally, the aged will retain a youthful look as long as they live. Should a man have debilitated himself with venery, he will be restored to his usual strength, if he confines himself to this as his only drink for nine days.

It will also cure impotence, in either sex, if used with food. When a couple are childless, let the wife, if young, use rosemary.

RUE : Gwenwynllys

Ruta graveolens

Rue is an aromatic perennial plant, native to southern Europe, introduced into Britain by the Romans. It is hardy and evergreen with alternate, bluish-green leaves which are tri-pinnate. They emit a powerful, disagreeable odour, with a very bitter and nauseous taste, it bears greenish-yellow flowers from June to September.

The actions of rue are anthelmintic, antispasmodic, emmenagogue, carminative and emetic in high dosage. The main uses for rue are to relieve gouty and rheumatic pains and to treat nervous heart problems, such as palpitations in women going through menopause.

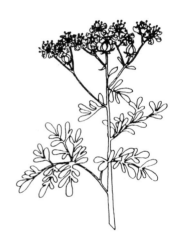

AN ANTIDOTE FOR POISONED FOOD
OR DRINK
pg. 309*53. Take rue, bruise well and pour white wine thereon (as much as will cover it), and if there is no wine, then ale, or mead; let the liquor and the herb be stirred well and strained. Let a draught of this be given to the patient in the morning fasting, and another in an hour, and he will be cured.

The name Ruta is from the Greek reuo (to set free), because the herb is so useful. The species name graveolens means strong smelling, from the Latin gravis, heavy, and oleo, smell. In the middle ages and later, it was considered a powerful defence against witches, and was used in many spells. It was also thought to bestow second sight.

SEA HOLLY, ERYNGO :
Morgelyn

Eryngium maritimum

This plant is seen only on the sand dunes of the sea shore. The smooth erect stem has a characteristic greenish-blue bloom, and grows to nearly one foot in height. The stiff, wavy leaves are divided into three lobes, with beautiful veins and sharp teeth at the margins. It blooms from July to September, producing pale blue flowers. The roots are used in herbalism.

Eryngo root is diaphoretic, diuretic and expectorant. In kidney disease, especially difficult and painful urination, it has long been used. As an expectorant it is especially indicated in debilitating chronic coughs. In conjunction with barberry bark it is indicated in jaundice and obstruction of the liver,

FOR A LIVID INFLAMMATION OF THE SKIN
pg. 344*262. Get eryngo, the leaves of the red alder, parsley, broom flowers, and the stinking iris, pound them well together and make into an ointment by means of butter and black soap. Anoint the painful part therewith, and it will heal it.

TO OBTAIN SLEEP
pg. 343*255. Take eryngo and mugwort, called orpin, mix with milk, and form into pills, administering unto the patient and will sleep presently.

From the 'Merry Wives of Windsor':

Falstaff: "My doe with the black scut! Let the sky rain potatoes; let it thunder to the tune of 'Greensleeves', hail kissing comfits and snow eringoes; let there come a tempest of provocation."

He meant candied eringoes. These were the candied roots of the eryngo, which were good for those 'that have no delight or appetite to venery'.

SHEPHERD'S PURSE :
Pwrs y Bugail

Capsella bursa-pastoris

Shepherd's purse is a very common plant of waste places, meadows, waysides and hedgerows. It has an erect stem which varies from a few inches to over a foot in height depending on the richness of the soil. The irregular lanceolate leaves also vary in size and shape with the plant's environment. Shepherd's purse is called from the resemblance of the flat seed-pouches to an old fashioned common leather purse. Another name for the plant is Mother's Heart.

The actions of the herb are astringent, vulnerary and diuretic. The tea is one of the best specifics for stopping haemorrhages of all kinds. It thus helps bleeding from wounds both internal and external. As an astringent, it has been used for diarrhoea, dysentery, piles, haematuria, nosebleed, etc. It is of great value in catarrhal conditions of the bladder and ureters, also in ulcerated conditions and abscess of the bladder. It increases the flow of urine.

FOR THE TOOTHACHE
pg. 308*48. Take shepherd's purse and pound
into a mass, then apply to the tooth.

SOUTHERNWOOD :
Lyiau'r Corph

Artemisia abrotanum

The plant is frequently seen in gardens, where it is cultivated for its delicate, graceful appearance and pleasant characteristic scent. It also grows wild on sandy heaths. The two foot high stems are at first prostrate, but become erect after producing, in August, small yellow flowers in leafy clusters. The greyish-green very slender leaves, are divided into many linear segments.

The actions of southernwood are emmenagogue, stimulant, anthelmintic and antispetic. The main use is as an emmenagogue, employed in menstrual obstruction frequently combined with Mugwort and Pennyroyal. The infusion should be used as boiling drives off the volatile oils. The powdered herb is sometimes used against worms in children, a teaspoonful being given in honey, morning and evening.

TO CURE ONE WHO TALKS IN HIS
SLEEP
pg. 308*46. Take southernwood, and pound it well, and add thereto some wine or old mead, strain well, and let the patient drink a portion thereof night and morning.

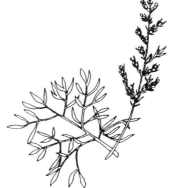

The name southernwood means the southern wormwood, as the plant is a native of southern Europe. Its folk uses are similar to those of wormwood.

The characteristic scent of the woods is due to an oil called Absinthol, used to flavour drinks such as Absinthe.

SUNDEW : Gwlithlys Mawr — *Drosera rotundifolia*

Sundew is an insectivorous plant well adapted to the infertile bogs and wet peaty places it inhabits. There is a basal rosette of nearly round, reddish leaves with long glandular hairs tipped with a sticky liquid which entraps insects. It has leafless flower stalks from 2 to 12 inches long which bear a spike of white five-petalled flowers. The entire plant is collected and dried during the flowering period of June to August.

Sundew finds its use in modern herbalism as a respiratory remedy. It is antispasmodic, demulcent, expectorant and appears to have a relaxing effect on the bronchial muscles. Use is made of it in the treatment of coughs, bronchitis, whooping cough and asthma, usually in combination with other remedies. The demulcent properties help with upset stomachs and gastric ulceration.

It was used by the Physicians of Myddfai as a wart remover in addition to being a pulmonary.

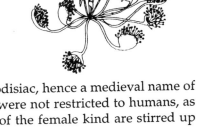

A folk use of sundew was as an aphrodisiac, hence a medieval name of youthwort. The aphrodisiac properties were not restricted to humans, as this quote from Gerard shows: "Cattle of the female kind are stirred up to lust by eating even of a small quantity.

TANSY : **Tanclys**

Tanacetum vulgare

This common wild plant was formerly cultivated in gardens, but is now rarely seen away from the borders of fields and waysides. The tough slightly ribbed stems reach a height of two or three feet, terminating in a bunch of yellow, flat, button-like flowers by which the plant may be easily recognised in July and August. An old country name for the plant was Batchelor's Buttons. Leaf stalks grow on alternate sides of the stem, the leaves themselves being six to eight inches long by about four inches broad and are deeply cut. The crushed leaves have a powerful aromatic smell.

Tansy is anthelmintic, tonic, stimulant and emmenagogue. It is perhaps the best remedy for worms in children. In moderate dosage it is a mild digestive agent and aid to regular period. However, in large amounts it can be a powerful irritant. Culpepper recommends it for women wanting to give birth. However, the herb was also used in large doses to induce abortion.

FOR AN OBSTINATE PAIN IN THE STOMACH
pg. 311*60. Drink the juice of the tansy in old ale, and you will be effectually cured.

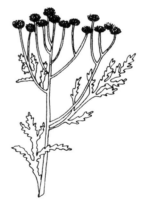

FOR ALL COMPLAINTS OF THE EYES, PARTICULARLY OPACITIES
pg. 334*197. Take wild or garden tansy, and boil well in white wine till the virtue of the herb is extracted; then remove from the fire, strain clean, and permit it to cool and clear. Afterwards take the clearest portion, and put some camphor therein, and leave till it is dissolved. Introduce some of this collyrium to the eye and whatever disease afflicts the eye, it will cure it.

THYME :
Teim, Gryw, Grywlys

Thymus serpyllum

This is the wild thyme, very similar to the common garden thyme, although smaller. It has numerous four-sided, woody stems, which grow procumbently. They grow to about 3 inches tall, depending on the conditions, and are finely hairy. The leaves are slightly downy on top, very downy underneath and are ovate to lanceolate in shape. The small bluish-purple, two-lipped flowers are whorled in dense head-like clusters, blooming from May to September.

Thyme is anthelmintic, antispasmodic, carminative, diaphoretic, expectorant and tonic. It is commonly used in throat and bronchial problems, including acute bronchitis, laryngitis and whooping cough, clearing mucus congestion from the lungs and respiratory passages. It makes a good tonic for the stomach and nerves, and is used in gastro-intestinal problems such as mild gastritis, enteritis stomach cramps and painful menstruation. A bath additive made from the decoction stimulates the flow of blood toward the surface of the body and alleviated nevous exhaustion. An infusion of the leaves is said to relieve the headache of a hangover.

FOR A COLD OR CATARRH, AND ALL KINDS OF PAIN IN THE SHOULDERS, ARMS AND LEGS
pg. 312*74. Take wild thyme, and bruise small, boil in the lees of strong ale till it is thickened, and apply thereto as hot as the patient can bear it. Let this be persevered in for nine days, and he will be effectually cured.

The name Thymus seems to be derived from the Greek word for sacrifice as the plant was used in temple offerings. It is best known for its fine fragrance and flavour, used extensively in cooking.

VALERIAN : **Llysiau Cadwgan** *Valeriana officinalis*

Valerian is found in damp places such as low-lying meadows and woods, about the banks of rivers and lakes, and in marshy, swampy ground generally. It is a handsome plant, growing from two to four feet high, and has stalks which are round, thick furrowed, and of a pale greenish colour. The leaves are pinnate with lance-shaped leaflets, growing opposite each other on the stem. The pink-white flowers, which appear from June to August, blossom in large tufts at the stalk head. A sweetish, disagreeable taste and unpleasant characteristic odour are given from the short thick, greyish rootsock. This is the part used medicinally.

Valerian is a powerful nervine tonic with antispasmodic and sedative properties. It is a powerful yet gentle sedative to the central nervous system and is used with great efficacy in hysteria, over-excitability, insomnia, etc. It is also useful when combined with other agents for the treatment of migraine. Its antispasmodic and carminative actions make it of service to cramp and intestinal colic. It has also proved useful in difficult and painful menstruation.

FOR AN IMPOSTUME (OR WHITLOW)
pg. 346*284. Take rue and wild valerian, pound them well and boil with rosin and yellow wax, apply as a plaster to the part. It is useful for all kinds of swellings in a finger or any other joint.

The name Valeriana is derived from the Latin valeo meaning to be well. This recognition of the herb's great healing power is reflected in a North Country name, Heal All.

VERVAIN :
Cas Gangythraul,
Llysiau'r Hudol, Y Dderwen Fendigaid

Verbena officinalis

Vervain is a rather uncommon plant of wayside and dry grassy places, especially on chalk and limestone. It has a tough, four-sided stem growing to about 18 inches high. The stem leaves grow opposite each other, they are stalkless and lobed. Small, pale lilac flowers bloom in May, along thin wiry spikes. The plant has no perfume, unlike the garden Verbenas, and is slightly bitter and astringent in taste. It must be picked before the flowers open and dried promptly.

This herb is a nervine, sedative, tonic with antispasmodic properties. It finds its main use today in the treatment of depression, melancholia and hysteria. It is thus a general tonic for the treatment of nervous disorders. It is a useful febrifuge in the early stages of a fever.

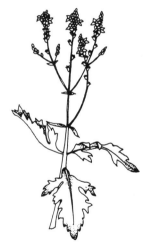

TO PREVENT DREAMS
pg. 338*220. Take the vervain, and hang about the man's neck, or give, him the juice on going to bed, and it will prevent his dreaming.

THE VIRTUES OF VERVAIN
pg. 448*798. The whole plant is good for all diseases proceeding from the poison of scrophula, whether affecting the lungs, liver, kidneys, brain, eyes, or any part. Gather this, and any other herb in the name of God, and give no heed to those who say that it should be gathered in the name of the devil.

The name Erbena was the classical Roman name for 'altar-plants' in general, and for this species in particular. It was one of the magic plants of the Druids, and magicians and sorcerers used it widely.

WOOD SAGE : **Dail y Cherwyn**   *Teucrium scorodonia*

Wood sage is found on dry hedgebanks and stone walls, in woods and on heaths especially on sandy soils. The whole plant is very similar to the cultivated garden sage.

The actions of wood sage are diuretic, diaphoretic, emmenagogue and tonic. It finds much use in the treatment of feverish colds, and also faulty menstruation when this is due to a chill. It is one of the many wound herbs found in nature, being especially good for cut blood vessels, ulcers, etc. It has been used as a tea against rheumatism. It also has bitter properties.

FOR THE GOUT
pg. 308*41. This disease is mostly confined to the feet and hands. Take wood sage, pellitory of the wall, wheatbran, cow's dung and salt, boil together in wine or cider vinegar and apply as a plaster to the painful part.

Before the use of hops was introduced into brewing, wood sage was often the bitter used.

WORMWOOD : **Wermwd Lwyd** *Artemisia absinthium*

Wormwood is a very distinctive plant found in waste places and waysides. The woody rootstock produces many bushy stems which may grow up to four feet high, bearing alternate tri-pinnate leaves covered in silky hairs. Numerous tiny yellow-green flower heads appear from July to October. The whole plant has a very stong aromatic smell and is exceedingly bitter.

Wormwood has wide medicinal applications, its actions include being a nervine tonic, digestive bitter, anthelminic, febrifuge, cholagogue, antiseptic and antispasmodic. It is primarily a stomach remedy used in cases of indigestion, gastric pain, lack of appetite, as well as the related problems of heartburn and flatulence. It is helpful in liver insufficiency because it stimulates liver and gall-bladder secretion. The flowering tops are used as an effective worm remedy.

FOR HYSTERIA
pg. 352*312. Get feverfew, wormwood, and the inner bark of ash, boil well in perennial spring water, strain, and drink, fasting for three mornings. This will procure you a recovery, so that you will not be afflicted ever again.

Many folk uses for wormwood are recorded. One such is an old love charm and another was a highly valued flea repeller.

YARROW :
Milddail, Llysiau Gwaedlif

Achillea millefilium

Yarrow, or milfoil, is a very common plant of fields, pastures, wayside and hedgerows. The light brown, creeping rootstock produces a round, smooth, pithy stem that branches near the top and may be smooth or hairy. The alternate leaves are deeply divided into many small segments. The flowers are small, white (occasionally pink or purplish), daisy-like, and bloom in dense, flattened, terminal heads, appearing at their best in July. The aerial parts are used in medicine.

This renowned herb has a number of actions; diaphoretic, astringent, antipyretic, hypotensive, diuretic and urinary antiseptic. The herb is extremely useful in colds and acute catarrhs of the respiratory tract generally. As it has the effect of opening the pores, and thereby permitting free perspiration, yarrow is taken at the beginning of influenza and other feverish conditions. As a very popular 'flu and cold remedy, it is often combined with Elder-flower and Peppermint. It has been found to have relevance to the treatment of high blood pressure. As an astringent it has value in the treatment of diarrhoea and dysentery. It is a useful diuretic with its antiseptic properties making it much used in cystitis.

FOR STRANGUARY AND THE STONE
pg. 322*125. Take the milfoil, and saxifrage, pound with warm water, and let the patient have this liquor for nine days as drink, nor let him, take any other drink, and by God's aid he will recover.

TO DESTROY PARASITES
pg. 433*758. Take milfoil, pound them well, and apply to the part affected.

Yarrow has been ascribed powerful magic properties, both for evil and against.

Index to Therapeutic Action of Herbs

Alteratives: Medicines which gradually alter and correct a poisoned condition of the blood stream, and restore healthier functioning.

Anthelmintics: Remedies for worms, including those agents which kill worms without necessarily causing their evacuation (vermicides), and those which expel them from the bowels, known as vermifuges.

Antilithic: An agent which reduces or suppresses urinary stones and acts to dissolve those already there.

Antiseptic: An agent for destroying or inhibiting pathogenic or putrefactive bacteria.

Antispasmodics: Reduce or prevent excessive involuntary muscular contractions.

Astringent: A remedy that contracts organic tissue, reducing secretions or discharges.

Bitter: Characterised by a bitter principle which acts on the mucous membranes of the mouth and stomach to increase appetite and promote digestion.

Demulcent: Soothes, softens and allays irritation of mucous membranes.

Diaphoretic: A remedy that induces an increased perspiration.

Diuretic: A herb that increases the secretion and expulsion of urine.

Emetic: A herb that brings about the evacuation of the stomach contents by vomiting.

Emmenagogues: Provokes and enhances the menstrual flow.

Emollients: Used extenally to soften and soothe.

Expectorant: A remedy that assists, by its influence on the respiratory passages, the increased secretion and ejection of mucus.

Febrifuges: Reduce temperature in fevers by enhancing the evaporation of perspiration.

Galactagogue: A herb that encourages or increases the secretion of milk.

Hypnotic: An agent that promotes or produces sleep.

Nervine: A remedy that has a calming or soothing effect on the nerves.

Oxytocic: An agent that stimulates contraction of the uterine muscles and so facilitates or speeds up childbirth.

Pectoral: A remedy for pulmonary or other chest diseases.

Sedative: A soothing herb that reduces nervousness, distress or irritation.

Stimulant: A herb that excites or quickens the activity of physiological processes.

Tonic: A remedy that strengthens or invigorates organs or the entire organism.

Vulnerary: A herb that promotes the healing of wounds.

Cathartic: Remedies that act to empty the bowels, laxative.

Cardiac: A Herb that stimulates or otherwise affects the heart.

Carminative: Remedies for the dispersal of gas in the intestine, and counteract the griping tendencies of certain laxatives.

Cholagogue: Herbs that increase the flow of bile into the intestines.

This little book tells you how the old physicians used herbs in Wales, and quote a lot about herbs today.

If you want to read further here are some good books:

Further Reading

GRIEVE, Mrs. M., *A Modern Herbal*, Penguin, 1976.

GRIGSON, Geoffrey, *The Englishman's Flora*, Paladin, 1975.

LEVY, Juliette de Bairacli, *Herbal Handbook For Everyone*, Faber, 1966.

LOEWENFELD, Claire, *Herb Gardening*, Faber, 1966.

LOEWENFELD and BACK, *Herbs for Health and Cookery*, Pan, 1965.

MABEY, Richard, *Food for Free*, Collins, 1972.

MABEY, Richard, *Plants with a Purpose*, Collins, 1977.

PUGHE, John, *The Physicians of Myddfai*, The Welsh Manuscript Society, 1861. Republished by Llanarch Enterprises, 1978, 1988 and 1989.

HARPER-SHOVE, *Medicinal Herbs*, Health Science Press, 1952.

LUST, John, *The Herb Book*, Balantine.

POTTERS CYCLOPAEDIA OF HERBS, Health Science Press.

FITTER, FITTER AND BLAMEY, *The Wild Flowers of Britain and Northern Europe*, Collins, 1974.

Useful Things

The following are things useful to be known by every Physician and even head of a family:

Infusion: Pouring water or other fluids in a boiling state upon herbs or whatever other ingredient that may be required.

Decoction: Boiling the herbs or ingredients in the water or fluid required.

Pottage or Porridge: Pouring boiling or cold water, or other fluid such as is required upon the herbs or other ingredients, leaving them to stand, then straining under a press.

Soakage: Pouring cold or boiling water, or other fluid on any substance capable of being influenced thereby, so as to become incorporated with what is poured thereupon.

Confection: Fluid mixed with powders or other substances capable of being administered as a draught.

Potion: A draught or fluid prepared according to art.

Essence: An amorphous or odoriferous substance which may be taken in a draught by mouth, or injected into the nostrils, ear, rectum or other parts.

Electuary: Substances incorporated into a dough so as to be eaten.

Constitution: The disposition which is in a man, or other living being or herb, or other matter; being their virtue inherent property, or nature.

Pills: Incorporated medical substances, formed into small balls so as to be taken at a gulp.

Bath: An infusion or decoction in which the patient or his limb is to be put.

Fomentation: To be applied as a wash to a hurt, whether hot or cold, as may be wanted.

Regimen: The food and drink as regulated by medical advice.

Weights and Measures

The following exhibits the weights and measures, which every Physician should employ, so that he may know certainly what proportions to use when necessary.

Weights and Measures of proportion
20 grains of wheat make one scruple
3 scruples make one drachm
8 drachms make one ounce

Fluid measures are arranged thus
Four podfuls make one spoonful
Four spoonfuls make one eggshellful
Four eggshellfuls make one cupful
Four cupfuls make one quart
Four quarts make one gallon
Four gallons make one pailful
Four pailfuls make one grenn (a large earthen-ware vessel)
Four grenns make one mydd
Four mydds make one myddi (a hogshead)

Also used are the following:
Two eggshells make half a pan
Two halfpans make a pan
Two pans make a phioled
Two phioleds, a cupful
Two cupfuls, a quart

The following are conjectural measures dependant upon the Physician's judgement.
Four grains of wheat make one pea
Four peas, one acorn
Four acorns, one pigeon's egg
Four pigeon's eggs, one hen's egg
Four hen eggs, one goose's egg
Four goose's eggs, one swan's egg.

Some Strange Remedies

We find throughout the Physicians of Myddfai some strange cures and some even stranger illnesses. Let us not ridicule them too much as we read for it must be remembered that every time has its superstitions, even our own.

How to be merry
pg. 52*58. If you would be at all times merry, eat saffron in meat or drink, and you will never be sad; but beware of eating over much, lest you should die of excessive joy.

To cure envy
pg. 52*59. If you would never be in an envious mood, drink as much as would fill an eggshell of the juice of the herb called wild clary, and you will not fall into an evil temper.

To preserve chastity
pg. 52*60. If you would always be chaste, eat daily some of the herb called hart's tongue, and you will never assent to suggestions of impurity.

A strange diagnostic of pregnancy
pg. 54*69. Whosoever would know whether a woman be with boy or girl, let him observe her sitting and standing, and if she moves her right foot first it signifies a son, but if the left, a daughter.

Strange diagnostic of virginity
pg. 54*70. If you distinguish between a wife and a virgin, scrape some jet into water and give it to her to drink. If she be a wife, she will without fail pass water, but if a virgin she will not have a more urgent call than usual.

To silence a cock
pg. 54*71. If you should wish a cock should not crow, anoint his crest with oil and he will be mute.

Reptiles in the stomach – to expel them
pg. 64*125. If a snake should enter a person's mouth, or there should be any other living reptiles in him, let him take wild chamomile (in powder) in wine, till it is thickened, drink the same and it will relieve him of them.

Intoxication
pg. 74*146. In order to be delivered from intoxication, drink saffron digested in spring water.

Chastity
pg. 75*150. If you would preserve yourself from unchaste thoughts and desires, eat rue in the morning.

To oblige a man to confess what he has done
pg. 453*803. Take a frog alive from the water, extract his tongue, and put him again in the water. Lay this same tongue upon the heart of a sleeping man, and he will confess his deeds to you in his sleep.

For the dropsy or hydrops
pg. 456*811. Rub young swallows with saffron, and in a short time the old swallows will bring them a stone; with this stone the patient will be cured of the hydrops.

For warts
pg. 456*812. Wash warts with the water from a font in which the seventh son of the same man and his wife is baptised.

A way in which a thing may be seen, which is invisible to others
pg. 456*814. Take the gall of a cat, and a hen's fat, mixing them together. Put this in your eyes, and you will see things which are invisble to others.

To enable a man to hold fire in his hand
pg. 457*815. Take marshmallows, and the white of two eggs, anoint your hands therewith, mixed together; then cover your hands with powdered alum, and you may handle fire without harm, or hold fire and hot iron in your hand without fear.

A charm for uterine disease, which was given by Rhiwallon the Physician to Gwyrvyl, daughter of Gruffydd ap Tewdwr
pg. 454*805. I adjure thee, thou diseased uterus, by the Father, the Son and the Holy Ghost, so that thou mightest not infect pain, nor have power (for the evil) in me Gwyrvyl, the daughter of Rhys, the servant of God, ether in my head, breast, stomach, or any other part of my body. Let God the Father prevail, let God the Son prevail, and let God the Holy Ghost prevail. Even so be it. Amen.

'Rachel' is one of the 20 tracks on our *Going, Going...* album from 2016. It was The Wedding Present's first double LP. The album is loosely linked with a road trip across the United States of America. It starts in Maine on the north east coast and ends in Santa Monica, California, but meanders through 20 states on the way. The title of each track is a location on that journey, and 'Rachel' is named after a town in Nevada that is quite near to Area 51 and, consequently, well known to UFO enthusiasts. I personally think it's one of the best pop songs that I've ever written. I love the verse chords because they are angular and slightly weird, but then it resolves into a chorus that is very sweet. It's just a simple little love song, really.

Going, Going... is actually a concept LP. I hate saying that because, when I think of concept albums, stuff like Rick Wakeman's *The Myths And Legends Of King Arthur And The Knights Of The Round Table* springs to mind. But there definitely is a concept here because the subject runs all the way through the tracks. In that respect it's like *Mini* or *Torino,* where the themes were, respectively, motor cars and an illicit love affair. Sometimes having a subject like that to work with can be very inspiring.

The lyrics on the album tell a story, which hopefully makes sense if you play the tracks in order. It's about a relationship that initially breaks up but which in the end is repaired. There is also a little side adventure on the way. 'Rachel' is the point in the saga where the protagonists get back together. The album title is from a Philip Larkin poem of which I'm fond, but it has nothing to do with the story on the record.

Early on, the lyrics I used for Wedding Present songs were very northern English in nature and told stories set in that particular part of the world. Over time, though, I have tried to change that to make it less specific, so I've written lyrics that could be placed anywhere. I wanted it not to matter who you were or where you were from, or even what the genders of the characters are. I wanted my lyrics to purely reflect the emotions of the protagonists, so that's what I aimed for after those early years. That said, *Take Fountain* includes a few references to Seattle and *El Rey* mentions LA because I was living in those places at the time I was writing the songs. 'Rachel' uses the American vernacular for 'railroad cars', which I would never personally use in conversation but which makes sense in this context.

I've always wanted the band to continually change and move on and try different ideas, regardless of what our fans think.

I agree with the notion that an artist shouldn't really be writing to please their devotees. I know it's now become a cliché, but I genuinely believe that the 'you should write for yourself and if other people like it, that's a bonus' rule is a good one. I never wanted to make the same album again and again, but if you want to be successful commercially, that's definitely the wrong way to go about it. It's like Weetabix. If someone goes out to buy a box of Weetabix, when they buy another box they don't want it tasting like Corn Flakes, they want Weetabix again. You can listen to all the Cinerama and Wedding Present albums and, if you discount my voice, it sounds like a different group every time. Of course it would have been more romantic to have those four lads who started in Leeds still working together over three decades later … like U2 or something. But I've definitely enjoyed moving on regularly and trying fresh ideas and having new people come in and say, 'I hate that stuff – let's do this.'

After all these years, I still consider Cinerama and The Wedding Present to be fragile little entities that could go up in smoke at any time and I think that anxiety is part of what drives me to continue, along with a fear of failure. But this is what I've always wanted to do and I am more than willing to put in the hard work. People are usually taken aback by how much actual time and effort I put into this. I'm your classic workaholic.

Ironically, although *Going, Going...* introduced features and styles that have never been used on Wedding Present records before, it almost feels like a nostalgic album to me. It's certainly lyrically one of my most personal records, along with *George Best* and *Take Fountain*. But there are also lots of little nods to the past. The strings from Cinerama are there, and then there are bits of *Bizarro* and *Seamonsters* because the guitarist Patrick Alexander consciously wanted to make those references. You can also hear *Saturnalia*-style experimentalism and the quirky pop of *Watusi*, and it's all held together by the epic production of Andrew Scheps, who reprised his *Valentina* role. In some ways I don't think it's too much of an exaggeration to describe *Going, Going...* as the ultimate Wedding Present record.

In 2017 we performed *Going, Going...* live at Cadogan Hall, which is the home of the Royal Philharmonic Orchestra in London. We had a full band, complemented by flute, brass, a string section and a 20-piece choir, and we supported ourselves as Cinerama. We projected the beautiful films that Jessica had made for each of the *Going, Going...* tracks onto a huge screen above the band. I think that this was probably the pinnacle of my live career.

There's a Wedding Present fan from Newcastle upon Tyne who I call 'The Postman'. He's not actually a postman but that's another story. He recently told me that he thought *Going, Going...* sounded like my 'swansong' and asked me if that was what it was going to be. I told him that, quite honestly, I didn't know.

Let's see if I write another.

THANKS

I would like to thank the following people, all of whom helped me in putting together this book: Mark Hodkinson, Jessica McMillan, Graham Williams, Jennie Roman, Terry de Castro, Lee Thacker, Richard Houghton, Danielle Wadey, Melanie Howard, Maria Forte, and Lloyd Bent.

ALSO PUBLISHED BY POMONA

Stuart Murdoch
THE CELESTIAL CAFÉ

Simon Armitage
BLACK ROSES
THE NOT DEAD

Dale Hibbert
BOY, INTERRUPTED

Bob Stanley
SLEEVENOTES

Joe Thompson
SLEEVENOTES

Mark Lanegan
SLEEVENOTES

www.pomonauk.com